NIST Special Publication 800-97

Establishing Wireless Robust Security Networks: A Guide to IEEE 802.11i

Recommendations of the National Institute of Standards and Technology

Sheila Frankel, Bernard Eydt, Les Owens, Karen Scarfone

COMPUTER SECURITY

Computer Security Division
Information Technology Laboratory
National Institute of Standards and Technology
Gaithersburg, MD 20899-8930

February 2007

U.S. Department of Commerce

Carlos M. Gutierrez, Secretary

Technology Administration

Robert C. Cresanti, Under Secretary of Commerce for Technology

National Institute of Standards and Technology

William Jeffrey, Director

Reports on Computer Systems Technology

The Information Technology Laboratory (ITL) at the National Institute of Standards and Technology (NIST) promotes the U.S. economy and public welfare by providing technical leadership for the nation's measurement and standards infrastructure. ITL develops tests, test methods, reference data, proof of concept implementations, and technical analysis to advance the development and productive use of information technology. ITL's responsibilities include the development of technical, physical, administrative, and management standards and guidelines for the cost-effective security and privacy of sensitive unclassified information in Federal computer systems. This Special Publication 800-series reports on ITL's research, guidance, and outreach efforts in computer security and its collaborative activities with industry, government, and academic organizations.

National Institute of Standards and Technology Special Publication 800-97
Natl. Inst. Stand. Technol. Spec. Publ. 800-97, 162 pages (February 2007)

Acknowledgements

The authors, Sheila Frankel and Karen Scarfone of the National Institute of Standards and Technology (NIST), and Bernard Eydt and Les Owens of Booz Allen Hamilton, wish to thank their colleagues who reviewed drafts of this document and contributed to its technical content. The authors would like to acknowledge Tim Grance, Lily Chen, Tim Polk and Randy Easter of NIST, and Alexis Feringa, Thomas Fuhrman, and Marc Stevens of Booz Allen Hamilton, for their keen and insightful assistance throughout the development of the document. The authors appreciate the detailed, perceptive in-depth comments provided by wireless experts Matthew Gast, Jesse Walker (Intel) and Nancy Cam-Winget (Cisco). The authors would also like to express their thanks to Bernard Aboba (Microsoft), Randy Chou (Aruba Networks), Ryon Coleman (3e Technologies), Paul Dodd (Boeing), Dean Farrington (Wells Fargo), Ben Halpert (Lockheed Martin), Criss Hyde, Timothy Kramer (Joint Systems Integration Command), W. J. Miller (MaCT), and Robert Smith (Juniper Networks) for their particularly valuable comments and suggestions.

Trademark Information

Microsoft, Windows, and Windows XP are either registered trademarks or trademarks of Microsoft Corporation in the United States and other countries.

Cisco and Cisco IOS are registered trademarks of Cisco Systems, Inc. in the United States and certain other countries.

Wi-Fi CERTIFIED is a trademark the Wi-Fi Alliance.

All other names are registered trademarks or trademarks of their respective companies.

Table of Contents

List of Appendices

List of Figures

List of Tables

Executive Summary

A wireless local area network (WLAN) enables access to computing resources for devices that are not physically connected to a network. WLANs typically operate over a fairly limited range, such as an office building or building campus, and usually are implemented as extensions to existing wired local area networks to enhance user mobility. This guide seeks to assist organizations in better understanding the most commonly used family of standards for WLANs—Institute of Electrical and Electronics Engineers (IEEE) 802.11—focusing on the security enhancements introduced in the IEEE 802.11i amendment. In particular, this guide explains the security features and provides specific recommendations to ensure the security of the operating environment.

Before IEEE 802.11i was finalized, IEEE 802.11 relied on a security method known as Wired Equivalent Privacy (WEP), which has several well-documented security problems. The IEEE 802.11i amendment introduces a range of new security features that are designed to overcome the shortcomings of WEP. It introduces the concept of a Robust Security Network (RSN), which is defined as a wireless security network that allows the creation of Robust Security Network Associations (RSNA) only. RSNAs are wireless connections that provide moderate to high levels of assurance against WLAN security threats through use of a variety of cryptographic techniques. This guide describes the operation of RSNs, including the steps needed to establish an RSNA and the flows of information between RSN components. The three types of RSN components are stations (STA), which are wireless endpoint devices such as laptops and wireless handheld devices (e.g. PDAs, text messaging devices and smart phones); access points (AP), which are network devices that allow STAs to communicate wirelessly and to connect to another network, typically an organization's wired infrastructure; and authentication servers (AS), which provide authentication services to STAs. STAs and APs are also found in pre-RSN WLANs, but ASs are a new WLAN component introduced by the RSN framework.

NIST recommends that Federal agencies implement the following recommendations to assist in establishing and maintaining robust security for their IEEE 802.11i-based WLANs. Personnel responsible for their implementation and maintenance should read the corresponding sections of the document to ensure they have an adequate understanding of important related issues.

This publication covers IEEE 802.11i-based wireless LANs only. It does not replace NIST Special Publication (SP) 800-48, *Wireless Network Security: 802.11, Bluetooth and Handheld Devices*, which addresses IEEE 802.11b and 802.11g-based wireless LANs, Bluetooth implementations, and wireless handheld devices (e.g., text messaging devices, PDAs, smart phones). Organizations with existing IEEE 802.11b or 802.11g implementations should continue to use the recommendations in SP 800-48 to secure them; they should also review this publication to understand the new IEEE 802.11i technology and how it addresses the shortcomings of the Wired Equivalent Privacy (WEP) protocol used to secure IEEE 802.11b and 802.11g networks. Organizations that are considering the deployment of new wireless LANs should be evaluating IEEE 802.11i-based products and following the recommendations for IEEE 802.11i implementations in this publication.

Organizations should ensure that all WLAN components use Federal Information Processing Standards (FIPS)-approved cryptographic algorithms to protect the confidentiality and integrity of WLAN communications.

The IEEE 802.11i amendment defines two data confidentiality and integrity protocols for RSNAs: Temporal Key Integrity Protocol (TKIP) and Counter Mode with Cipher Block Chaining Message Authentication Code Protocol (CCMP). This guide discusses both protocols at length, as well as the cryptographic keys created and used by these protocols. Federal agencies are required to use

FIPS-approved cryptographic algorithms that are contained in FIPS-validated cryptographic modules.[1] Of WEP, TKIP, and CCMP, only CCMP uses a core cryptographic algorithm that is FIPS-approved, the Advanced Encryption Standard (AES). For other security features, CCMP offers stronger assurance than WEP and TKIP. Accordingly, NIST requires the use of CCMP for securing Federal agencies' IEEE 802.11-based WLANs. For legacy IEEE 802.11 equipment that does not provide CCMP, auxiliary security protection is required; one possibility is the use of an IPsec VPN, using FIPS-approved cryptographic algorithms. NIST SP 800-48 contains specific recommendations for securing legacy IEEE 802.11 implementations.

Organizations should select IEEE 802.11 RSN authentication methods for their environment carefully.

IEEE 802.11 RSN uses the Extensible Authentication Protocol (EAP) for the authentication phase of establishing an RSNA. EAP supports a wide variety of authentication methods, also called EAP methods. They include authentication based on passwords, certificates, smart cards, and tokens. EAP methods also can include combinations of authentication techniques, such as a certificate followed by a password, or the option of using either a smart card or a token. This flexibility allows EAP to integrate with nearly any environment to which a WLAN might connect. Organizations have considerable discretion in choosing which EAP methods to employ; a poor EAP method choice or implementation could seriously weaken an IEEE 802.11 RSN's protections.

Because of the extensible nature of EAP, dozens of EAP methods exist, and others are being developed continually. However, many EAP methods do not satisfy the necessary security requirements for WLANs; for example, EAP methods that do not generate cryptographic keying material cannot be used for WLANs. In general, the current EAP methods that can satisfy WLAN security requirements are based on the Transport Layer Security (TLS) protocol. A primary distinction between TLS-based EAP methods is the level of public key infrastructure (PKI) support required; the EAP-TLS method requires an enterprise PKI implementation and certificates deployed to each STA, while most other TLS methods require certificates on each AS only. Organizations should use the EAP-TLS method whenever possible.

Because some EAP methods are not yet official standards and new methods are being developed, organizations are encouraged to obtain the latest available information on EAP methods and standards when planning an IEEE 802.11 RSN implementation. Additionally, organizations should ensure that the cryptographic modules implementing the TLS algorithm for each product under consideration are FIPS-validated.

Before selecting WLAN equipment, organizations should review their existing identity management infrastructure, authentication requirements, and security policy to determine the EAP method or methods that are most appropriate in their environments, then purchase systems that support the chosen EAP methods, and implement and maintain them carefully. This publication provides detailed guidance on planning EAP implementations. It discusses the most common EAP methods, explains how organizations can select EAP methods, and examines additional EAP security considerations.

---

[1] Information about NIST's Cryptographic Module Validation program can be found at http://csrc.nist.gov/cryptval/140-2.htm FIPS PUB 140-2 (http://csrc.nist.gov/publications/fips/fips140-2/fips1402.pdf) describes the generic security requirements; the implementation guide (http://csrc.nist.gov/cryptval/140-1/FIPS1402IG.pdf) includes specific implementation guidance for IEEE 802.11 Lists of FIPS-approved cryptographic products can be found at http://csrc.nist.gov/cryptval/140-1/1401val.htm

Organizations should integrate their existing authentication technology with their IEEE 802.11 RSN WLAN to the extent feasible.

Although the RSN framework supports the use of pre-shared keys (PSK), organizations should choose to implement the IEEE 802.1X standard and EAP for authentication instead of using PSKs because of the resources needed for proper PSK administration and the security risks involved. IEEE 802.1X and EAP authentication requires an organization to use an AS, which may necessitate the use of a PKI. An organization that already has ASs for Web, e-mail, file and print services, and other authentication needs, should consider integrating this technology into its RSN solution. Most leading network operating systems and directory solutions offer the support needed for RSN integration.

Organizations should ensure that the confidentiality and integrity of communications between access points and authentication servers are protected sufficiently.

The data confidentiality and integrity protocol (such as CCMP) used by an IEEE 802.11 RSN protects communications between STAs and APs. However, IEEE 802.11 and its related standards explicitly state that protection of the communications between the AP and AS is out of their scope. Therefore, organizations deploying RSNs should ensure that communications between each AP and its corresponding ASs are protected sufficiently through cryptography. Also, because of the importance of the ASs, organizations should pay particular attention to establishing and maintaining their security through operating system configuration, firewall rules, and other security controls.

Organizations establishing IEEE 802.11 RSNs should use technologies that have the appropriate security certification from NIST and interoperability certification from the Wi-Fi Alliance.

To implement IEEE 802.11 RSNs, organizations may need to update or replace existing IEEE 802.11 equipment and software that cannot support RSNAs, as well as purchase additional equipment. The Wi-Fi Alliance, a non-profit industry consortium of WLAN equipment and software vendors, has established the Wi-Fi Protected Access 2 (WPA2) certification program to give consumers of WLAN products assurance that their IEEE 802.11i systems can interoperate with similar equipment from other vendors. Federal agencies should procure WPA2 products that use FIPS-approved encryption algorithms and have been FIPS-validated. Organizations that plan to use authentication servers as part of their IEEE 802.11 RSN implementations should procure products with the WPA2 Enterprise level certification. Also, because the WPA2 certification is expanded periodically to test for interoperability with additional EAP methods, organizations should obtain the latest WPA2 information before making procurement decisions.

Organizations should ensure that WLAN security considerations are incorporated into each phase of the WLAN life cycle when establishing and maintaining IEEE 802.11 RSNs.

This guide presents extensive guidance on IEEE 802.11 RSN planning and implementation. It describes a life cycle model for WLANs and presents best practice recommendations related to WLAN security for each phase in the life cycle. WLAN security considerations for each phase include the following:

- **Phase 1: Initiation**. This phase includes the tasks that an organization should perform before it starts to design its WLAN solution. These include developing a WLAN use policy, performing a WLAN risk assessment, and specifying business and functional requirements for the solution, such as mandating RSNAs for all WLAN connections.

- **Phase 2: Acquisition/Development.** For the purposes of this guide, the Acquisition/Development phase is split into the following two phases:

- **Phase 2a: Planning and Design**. In this phase, WLAN network architects specify the technical characteristics of the WLAN solution, such as authentication methods, and related network components, such as firewall rulesets. The WLAN network architects should also conduct a site survey to help determine the architecture of the solution and how the WLAN should be integrated with the existing authentication infrastructure, including PKI.

- **Phase 2b: Procurement**. This phase involves specifying the number and type of WLAN components that must be purchased, the feature sets they must support (e.g., FIPS-validated encryption modules), and any certifications they must hold (e.g., WPA2 Enterprise).

- **Phase 3: Implementation**. In this phase, procured equipment is first configured to meet operational and security requirements, and then installed and activated on a production network, with appropriate event logging enabled.

- **Phase 4: Operations/Maintenance**. This phase includes security-related tasks that an organization should perform on an ongoing basis once the WLAN is operational, including patching, periodic security assessment, log reviews, and incident handling.

- **Phase 5: Disposition.** This phase encompasses tasks that occur after a system or its components have been retired, including preserving information to meet legal requirements, sanitizing media that might contain sensitive material, and disposing of equipment properly.

1. Introduction

1.1 Authority

The National Institute of Standards and Technology (NIST) developed this document in furtherance of its statutory responsibilities under the Federal Information Security Management Act (FISMA) of 2002, Public Law 107-347.

NIST is responsible for developing standards and guidelines, including minimum requirements, for providing adequate information security for all agency operations and assets; but such standards and guidelines shall not apply to national security systems. This guideline is consistent with the requirements of the Office of Management and Budget (OMB) Circular A-130, Section 8b(3), "Securing Agency Information Systems," as analyzed in A-130, Appendix IV: Analysis of Key Sections. Supplemental information is provided in A-130, Appendix III.

This guideline has been prepared for use by Federal agencies. It may be used by nongovernmental organizations on a voluntary basis and is not subject to copyright, though attribution is desired.

Nothing in this document should be taken to contradict standards and guidelines made mandatory and binding on Federal agencies by the Secretary of Commerce under statutory authority, nor should these guidelines be interpreted as altering or superseding the existing authorities of the Secretary of Commerce, Director of the OMB, or any other Federal official.

1.2 Purpose and Scope

This publication seeks to assist organizations in understanding, selecting, and implementing technologies based on Institute of Electrical and Electronics Engineers (IEEE) 802.11i, part of the IEEE 802.11 family of wireless networking standards.[2] The document explains at length the security features and capabilities associated with IEEE 802.11i through its framework for Robust Security Networks (RSN), and provides extensive guidance on the planning and deployment of RSNs. The document also discusses previous IEEE 802.11 security measures and their shortcomings.

1.3 Audience

This document has been created for those who are responsible for ensuring the security of wireless local area networks (WLAN). The guide should also be useful for network and security engineers and administrators who are responsible for designing, implementing, securing, and maintaining IEEE 802.11i implementations.

1.4 Document Structure

The remainder of this document is organized into the following nine major sections:

- Section 2 provides an overview of wireless networking, focusing on the IEEE 802.11 family of WLAN standards, and explains the basic IEEE 802.11 WLAN components and architectural models.

---

[2] By the end of 2006, 802 11i will no longer exist, because it is being rolled into the base standard At that time, the reference is expected to be IEEE 802 11:2006

- Section 3 gives an overview of IEEE 802.11 security, including a review of the security features and weaknesses of IEEE 802.11 before the introduction of the IEEE 802.11i amendment. It also introduces the major security-related components that are defined in IEEE 802.11i.

- Section 4 introduces the concepts of Robust Security Networks (RSN) and Robust Security Network Associations (RSNA). It also discusses the RSN data confidentiality and integrity protocols, and the cryptographic keys created and used by these protocols.

- Section 5 describes the five phases that occur during RSN communication, starting with the discovery of a WLAN and ending in connection termination. It also discusses the types of frames used to carry information between RSN components, and depicts the flows of frames between components during each phase of RSN operation.

- Section 6 provides guidance on planning an Extensible Authentication Protocol (EAP) implementation, which is necessary for most enterprise RSN deployments. It discusses the most common EAP methods, explains how organizations can select EAP methods appropriate to their environments, examines additional EAP security considerations, and introduces the EAP architectural model and related support requirements.

- Section 7 describes FIPS 140-2 certification as it applies to 802.11 wireless networks. It also provides an overview of the security specifications developed by the Wi-Fi Alliance, which conducts a certification program for the interoperability of WLAN products. The certifications are intended to help organizations select WLAN products that can support RSNs.

- Section 8 presents best practice recommendations related to WLAN security.

- Section 9 presents three case studies that illustrate how organizations might plan, design, and implement RSNs in different scenarios, such as migrating a WLAN from pre-RSN to RSN technology, and designing a new WLAN that meets RSN requirements.

- Section 10 summarizes the major concepts and recommendations presented in Sections 2 through 8 of the document.

- Section 11 provides a brief overview of possible extensions to IEEE 802.11i that are currently being developed.

The document also contains appendices with supporting material. Appendix A contains an acronym list. Appendix B lists the document's references and other sources of information that may be of interest to readers. Appendix C identifies online resources that may be helpful for better understanding IEEE 802.11i and IEEE 802.11i security.

1.5   How to Navigate This Document

This document is intended to be used by readers with various levels of experience and technical knowledge, as well as different interests in IEEE 802.11i. For example, computer security program managers might want to learn the basic IEEE 802.11i concepts and terminology, while network and security engineers might want to know as many details about the technical configuration of IEEE 802.11i technologies as possible. The lists below provide general recommendations as to which sections and sub-sections of the guide should be read, based on the reader's objectives. Readers who are unsure about the relevance or appropriateness of a particular section should read its introduction and summary to gain a better understanding of what the section contains.

■ **Practical Guidance on Implementing IEEE 802.11i Security.** Readers who want to know how to implement IEEE 802.11i security should read Sections 7 and 8, as well as the Section 9 case studies that most closely match their needs.

■ **Basic Knowledge of IEEE 802.11i and RSNs.** Readers who want to understand the basics of IEEE 802.11i and RSNs, and are not interested in detailed technical explanations of protocols and RSN operation, should do the following:

  – Read Sections 2 and 3.

  – Skim Sections 4 through 6, reading each section summary carefully.

■ **Detailed Knowledge of IEEE 802.11i and RSNs.** Readers who are seeking solid knowledge of IEEE 802.11i should read Sections 2 through 7, skimming any parts that contain familiar content.

■ **All the Details of IEEE 802.11i and RSNs**. Readers who want to learn as much as possible should read the entire document.

This page has been left blank intentionally.

2. Overview of Wireless Networking

Wireless networking enables devices with wireless capabilities to use computing resources without being physically connected to a network. The devices simply need to be within a certain distance (known as the *range*) of the wireless network infrastructure. A wireless local area network (WLAN) is a group of wireless networking nodes within a limited geographic area that is capable of radio communications. WLANs are typically used by devices within a fairly limited range, such as an office building or building campus, and are usually implemented as extensions to existing wired local area networks to provide enhanced user mobility.

Since the beginning of wireless networking, many standards and technologies have been developed for WLANs. One of the most active standards organizations that address wireless networking is the Institute of Electrical and Electronics Engineers (IEEE). This section of the guide provides an overview of wireless networking and focuses on the IEEE 802.11 family of WLAN standards. Section 2.1 discusses the history of IEEE 802.11 and provides examples of alternative wireless networking standards.[3] Section 2.2 explains the basic IEEE 802.11 WLAN components and architectural models, which lays a foundation for subsequent sections of the guide. Readers who are already familiar with the basics of WLANs and IEEE 802.11 might wish to skip this section.

2.1 History of Wireless Networking Standards

WLAN technologies were first available in late 1990, when vendors began introducing products that operated within the 900 megahertz (MHz) frequency band. These solutions, which used non-standard, proprietary designs, provided data transfer rates of approximately 1 megabit per second (Mbps). This was significantly slower than the 10 Mbps speed provided by most wired local area networks (LAN) at that time. In 1992, vendors began selling WLAN products that used the 2.4 gigahertz (GHz) band. Although these products provided higher data transfer rates than 900 MHz band products, they also used proprietary designs. The need for interoperability among different brands of WLAN products led to several organizations developing wireless networking standards. Section 2.1.1 describes the IEEE 802.11 family of standards. Section 2.1.2 discusses work from the Wi-Fi Alliance that is closely related to IEEE 802.11, and Section 2.1.3 briefly highlights other wireless networking standards.

2.1.1 IEEE 802.11 Standards

In 1997, IEEE ratified the 802.11 standard for WLANs. The IEEE 802.11 standard supports three transmission methods, including radio transmission within the 2.4 GHz band. In 1999, IEEE ratified two amendments to the 802.11 standard—802.11a and 802.11b—that define radio transmission methods, and WLAN equipment based on IEEE 802.11b quickly became the dominant wireless technology. IEEE 802.11b equipment transmits in the 2.4 GHz band, offering data rates of up to 11 Mbps. IEEE 802.11b was intended to provide performance, throughput, and security features comparable to wired LANs. In 2003, IEEE released the 802.11g amendment, which specifies a radio transmission method that uses the 2.4 GHz band and can support data rates of up to 54 Mbps. Additionally, IEEE 802.11g-compliant products are backward compatible with IEEE 802.11b-compliant products. Table 2-1 compares the basic characteristics of IEEE 802.11, 802.11a, 802.11b, and 802.11g. 802.11 wireless networking is also known as Wi-Fi ®.

---

[3]   For more information on the IEEE 802 11 standards and other aspects of wireless network security, see NIST Special Publication (SP) 800-48, *Wireless Network Security: 802.11, Bluetooth and Handheld Devices* (http://csrc nist gov/publications/nistpubs/800-48/NIST_SP_800-48 pdf)

Table 2-1. Summary of IEEE 802.11 WLAN Technologies

IEEE Standard or Amendment	Maximum Data Rate	Typical Range	Frequency Band	Comments
802.11	2 Mbps	50-100 meters	2.4 GHz	
802.11a	54 Mbps	50-100 meters	5 GHz	Not compatible with 802.11b
802.11b	11 Mbps	50-100 meters	2.4 GHz	Equipment based on 802.11b has been the dominant WLAN technology
802.11g	54 Mbps	50-100 meters	2.4 GHz	Backward compatible with 802.11b

Table 2-1 does not include all current and pending 802.11 amendments. For example, in November 2005, IEEE ratified IEEE 802.11e, which provides quality of service enhancements to IEEE 802.11 that improve the delivery of multimedia content. The IEEE 802.11n project is specifying IEEE 802.11 enhancements that will enable data throughput of at least 100 Mbps. Final working group approval is expected in January 2008, with an interim Wi-Fi certification sometime in 2007; products based on the 802.11n draft are currently available.

The IEEE 802.11 variants[4] listed in Table 2-1 all include security features known collectively as Wired Equivalent Privacy (WEP) that are supposed to provide a level of security comparable to that of wired LANs. As described in Section 3, IEEE 802.11 configurations that rely on WEP have several well-documented security problems. The IEEE acknowledged the scope of the problems and developed short-term and long-term strategies for rectifying the situation. In June 2004, the IEEE finalized the 802.11i amendment, which is designed to overcome the shortcomings of WEP. IEEE 802.11i specifies security components that work in conjunction with all the IEEE 802.11 radio standards, such as IEEE 802.11a, 802.11b, and 802.11g; any future 802.11 physical layer will also be compatible with 802.11i. Section 3 presents additional information on the IEEE 802.11i amendment.

2.1.2 Wi-Fi Alliance Certification

While IEEE was examining the shortcomings of IEEE 802.11 security and starting to develop the 802.11i amendment, a non-profit industry consortium of WLAN equipment and software vendors called the Wi-Fi Alliance developed an interoperability certification program for WLAN products.[5] The Wi-Fi Alliance felt it was necessary to create an interim solution that could be deployed using existing IEEE 802.11 hardware while IEEE worked on finalizing the 802.11i amendment. Accordingly, the Alliance created Wi-Fi Protected Access (WPA), which was published in October 2002; it is essentially a subset of the draft IEEE 802.11i requirements available at that time. The most significant difference between WPA and the IEEE 802.11i drafts is that WPA does not require support for Advanced Encryption Standard (AES), a strong encryption algorithm, because many existing IEEE 802.11 hardware components cannot support computationally intensive encryption without additional hardware components.[6]

---

[4] For information on other IEEE 802.11 amendments (e g , 802.11e, 802.11n), visit
http://grouper.ieee.org/groups/802/11/QuickGuide_IEEE_802_WG_and_Activities.htm
[5] For more information on the Wi-Fi Alliance, visit their Web site at http://www.wi-fi.org/
[6] Federal agencies are required to use encryption algorithms that are Federal Information Processing Standards (FIPS) approved FIPS 140-2, *Security Requirements for Cryptographic Modules*, is available at
http://csrc.nist.gov/publications/fips/fips140-2/fips1402.pdf

In conjunction with the ratification of the IEEE 802.11i amendment, the Wi-Fi Alliance introduced WPA2, its term for interoperable equipment that is capable of supporting IEEE 802.11i requirements.[7] The Wi-Fi Alliance began testing IEEE 802.11i products for WPA2 certification shortly after the IEEE 802.11i amendment was finalized. Section 7 provides more information on WPA and WPA2.

2.1.3 Other Wireless Standards

In addition to the IEEE 802.11 and WPA standards, other wireless standards are also in use. These standards are unrelated to IEEE 802.11, but are presented in this section to provide context and illustrate how IEEE 802.11 and other standards meet different needs. The following list describes the major wireless architecture categories and provides examples of selected key current and emerging wireless standards.

- **Wireless personal area networks (WPAN):** small-scale wireless networks that require little or no infrastructure. A WPAN is typically used by a few devices in a single room instead of connecting the devices with cables. For example, WPANs can provide print services or enable a wireless keyboard or mouse to communicate with a computer. Examples of WPAN standards include the following:

    - **IEEE 802.15.1 (Bluetooth)**. This WPAN standard is designed for wireless networking between small portable devices. The original Bluetooth operated at 2.4 GHz and has a maximum data rate of approximately 720 kilobits per second (Kbps); Bluetooth 2.0 can reach 3 Mbps.[8]

    - **IEEE 802.15.3 (High-Rate Ultrawideband; WiMedia, Wireless USB)**. This is a low-cost, low power consumption WPAN standard that uses a wide range of GHz frequencies to avoid interference with other wireless transmissions. It can achieve data rates of up to 480 Mbps over short ranges and can support the full range of WPAN applications. One expected use of this technology is the ability to detect shapes through physical barriers such as walls and boxes, which could be useful for applications ranging from law enforcement to search and rescue operations.

    - **IEEE 802.15.4 (Low-Rate Ultrawideband; ZigBee)**. This is a simple protocol for lightweight WPANs.[9] It is most commonly used for monitoring and control products, such as climate control systems and building lighting.

- **Wireless local area networks (WLAN).** IEEE 802.11 is the dominant WLAN standard, but others have also been defined. For example, the European Telecommunications Standards Institute (ETSI) has published the **High Performance Radio Local Area Network (HIPERLAN)** WLAN standard that transmits data in the 5 GHz band and operates at data rates of approximately 23.5 Mbps.[10] However, HIPERLAN appears to have been supplanted by IEEE 802.11 in the commercial arena.

- **Wireless metropolitan area networks (WMAN):** networks that can provide connectivity to users located in multiple facilities that are generally within a few miles of each other. Many WMAN implementations provide wireless broadband access to customers in metropolitan areas. For example, IEEE 802.16e (better known as WiMAX) is a WMAN standard that transmits in the

---

[7] WPA2 does not test interoperability of ad hoc operation (IBSS) or pre-authentication for IEEE 802 11i
[8] More information on Bluetooth is available from NIST SP 800-48, *Wireless Network Security: 802.11, Bluetooth and Handheld Devices*, located at http://csrc nist gov/publications/nistpubs/800-48/NIST_SP_800-48 pdf
[9] The ZigBee Alliance Web site (http://www zigbee org/) has additional information on ZigBee
[10] For more information, visit http://portal etsi org/radio/HiperLAN/HiperLAN asp

10 to 66 GHz band range.[11] An IEEE 802.16a addendum allows for large data transmissions with minimal interference. WiMAX provides throughput of up to 75 Mbps, with a range of up to 30 miles for fixed line-of-site communication. However, there is generally a tradeoff; 75 Mbps throughput is possible at half a mile, but at 30 miles the throughput is much lower.

■ **Wireless wide area networks (WWAN):** networks that connect individuals and devices over large geographic areas, often globally. WWANs are typically used for cellular voice and data communications, as well as satellite communications.

2.2 IEEE 802.11 Network Components and Architectural Models

IEEE 802.11 has two fundamental architectural components, as follows:

■ **Station (STA).** A *STA* is a wireless endpoint device. Typical examples of STAs are laptop computers, personal digital assistants (PDA), mobile phones, and other consumer electronic devices with IEEE 802.11 capabilities.

■ **Access Point (AP).** [12] An *AP* logically connects STAs with a distribution system (DS), which is typically an organization's wired infrastructure. APs can also logically connect wireless STAs with each other without accessing a distribution system.

The IEEE 802.11 standard also defines the following two WLAN design structures or configurations, which are discussed in more detail in Sections 2.2.1 and 2.2.2:

■ **Ad Hoc Mode.** The *ad hoc mode* does not use APs. Ad hoc mode is sometimes referred to as infrastructureless because only peer-to-peer STAs are involved in the communications.

■ **Infrastructure Mode.** In *infrastructure mode*, an AP connects wireless STAs to each other or to a distribution system, typically a wired network. Infrastructure mode is the most commonly used mode for WLANs.

2.2.1 Ad Hoc Mode

The ad hoc mode (or topology) is depicted conceptually in Figure 2-1. This mode of operation, also known as *peer-to-peer mode*, is possible when two or more STAs are able to communicate directly to one another. Figure 2-1 shows three devices communicating with each other in a peer-to-peer fashion without any infrastructure. A set of STAs configured in this ad hoc manner is known as an *independent basic service set* (IBSS).

Today, a STA is most often thought of as a simple laptop with an inexpensive network interface card (NIC) that provides wireless connectivity; however, many other types of devices could also be STAs. In Figure 2-1, the STAs in the IBSS are a mobile phone, a laptop, and a PDA. IEEE 802.11 and its variants continue to increase in popularity; scanners, printers, digital cameras and other portable devices can also be STAs. The circular shape in Figure 2-1 depicts the IBSS. It is helpful to consider this as the radio frequency coverage area within which the stations can remain in communication. A fundamental property of IBSS is that it defines no routing or forwarding, so, based on the bare IEEE 802.11i spec, all the devices must be within radio range of one another.

---

[11] Visit the WiMAX Forum located at http://www.wimaxforum.org/home/ for more information on WiMAX
[12] Technically, APs are also STAs. Some literature distinguishes between AP STAs and non-AP STAs. In this document, the term STA refers to non-AP STAs only.

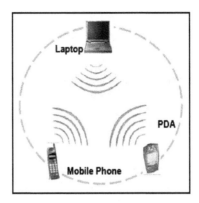

Figure 2-1. IEEE 802.11 Ad Hoc Mode

One of the key advantages of ad hoc WLANs is that theoretically they can be formed any time and anywhere, allowing multiple users to create wireless connections cheaply, quickly, and easily with minimal hardware and user maintenance. In practice, many different types of ad hoc networks are possible, and the IEEE 802.11 specification allows all of them. Since it does not give the details of how to form a network, but rather only how to establish the links in a network, ad hoc mode as specified by 802.11 is incomplete for any particular use. This means that different products built on it typically are not interoperable, because there has not yet been standardization on any of these possible networks.

An ad hoc network can be created for many reasons, such as allowing the sharing of files or the rapid exchange of e-mail. However, an ad hoc WLAN cannot communicate with external networks. A further complication is that an ad hoc network can interfere with the operation of an AP-based infrastructure mode network (see next section) that exists within the same wireless space.

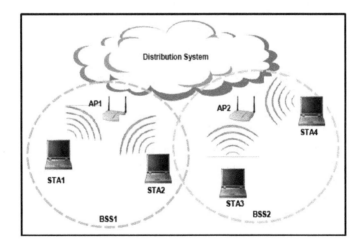

Figure 2-2. IEEE 802.11 Infrastructure Mode

2.2.2 Infrastructure Mode

In infrastructure mode, an IEEE 802.11 WLAN comprises one or more Basic Service Sets (BSS), the basic building blocks of a WLAN. A *BSS* includes an AP and one or more STAs. The AP in a BSS connects the STAs to the DS. The DS is the means by which STAs can communicate with the organization's wired LANs and external networks such as the Internet. The IEEE 802.11 infrastructure mode is depicted in Figure 2-2.

The DS and use of multiple BSSs and their associated APs allow for the creation of wireless networks of arbitrary size and complexity. In the IEEE 802.11 specification, this type of multi-BSS network is referred to as an *extended service set* (ESS). Figure 2-3 conceptually depicts a network with both wired and wireless capabilities. It shows three APs with their corresponding BSSs, which comprise an ESS; the ESS is attached to the wired infrastructure. In turn, the wired infrastructure is connected through a perimeter firewall to the Internet. This architecture could permit various STAs, such as laptops and PDAs, to provide Internet connectivity for their users.

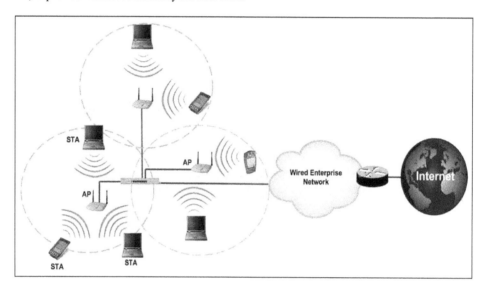

Figure 2-3. Extended Service Set in an Enterprise

2.3 Summary

WLANs are usually implemented as extensions to existing wired LANs, and are used by devices within a fairly limited range, such as an office building. The need for interoperability among different brands of WLAN products led to the development of various WLAN standards. IEEE 802.11 is the dominant WLAN standard. At the time that the IEEE 802.11i amendment was finalized, WLAN equipment based on IEEE 802.11b was the most popular; it was intended to provide performance, throughput, and security features comparable to wired LANs. Unfortunately, IEEE 802.11 technologies that rely on WEP have several well-documented security problems, which are described in Section 3. To address these, IEEE amended 802.11 with 802.11i, which was approved in June 2004. The subsequent sections of this guide cover IEEE 802.11i features and security considerations in depth.

This section also explains the basic IEEE 802.11 network components and architectural models, as a foundation for understanding other sections of this guide. The major concepts introduced in this section are as follows:

- **Station (STA).** A *STA* is a wireless endpoint device,[13] such as a laptop, PDA, or mobile phone.

- **Access Point (AP).** An *AP* logically connects STAs with a distribution system, which is typically an organization's wired network infrastructure. APs can also logically connect wireless STAs with each other without accessing a distribution system.

- **Ad Hoc Mode.** This is a wireless network configuration that does not use APs; STAs communicate directly with each other.

- **Infrastructure Mode.** This wireless network configuration requires APs and is the most commonly used mode for WLANs. All STAs connect with an AP, and the AP transfers frames among the STAs and the distribution system.

- **Independent Basic Service Set (IBSS).** An IBSS is a set of STAs configured in ad hoc mode.

- **Basic Service Set (BSS).** A BSS is composed of an AP and one or more STAs configured in infrastructure mode. Each of the STAs associate directly with the AP. A BSS is the basic building block of a WLAN.

- **Distribution System (DS).** A DS is an infrastructure, typically a wired LAN, that connects individual BSSs to each other.

- **Extended Service Set (ESS).** An ESS is a WLAN comprising more than one BSS connected by a DS.

---

[13] Technically, a STA is a wireless network interface implementation It is distinct from the device that will provide an application using the network interface (such as a laptop or PDA)

This page has been left blank intentionally.

3. Overview of IEEE 802.11 Security

This section provides an overview of IEEE 802.11 security. It begins by explaining the main security concerns and threats against WLANs. Next, it reviews the security features and weaknesses of IEEE 802.11 before the introduction of the IEEE 802.11i amendment to the IEEE 802.11 WLAN standard, and the IEEE 802.11i framework for Robust Security Networks (RSN). The review of pre-RSN IEEE 802.11 security demonstrates the shortcomings of the standard and the motivation behind the development of the IEEE 802.11i amendment and the RSN framework, which is intended to provide strong authentication for WLAN devices and strong protection for WLAN communications. The section then introduces the major security-related components that are defined in the IEEE 802.11i amendment.

This publication covers IEEE 802.11i-based wireless LANs only. It does not replace NIST Special Publication (SP) 800-48, *Wireless Network Security: 802.11, Bluetooth and Handheld Devices*, which addresses IEEE 802.11b and 802.11g-based wireless LANs, Bluetooth implementations, and wireless handheld devices (e.g., text messaging devices, PDAs, smart phones). Organizations with existing IEEE 802.11b or 802.11g implementations should continue to use the recommendations in SP 800-48 to secure them;[14] they should also review this publication to understand the new IEEE 802.11i technology and how it addresses the shortcomings of the WEP protocol used to secure IEEE 802.11b and 802.11g networks. Organizations that are considering the deployment of new wireless LANs should be evaluating IEEE 802.11i-based products and following the recommendations for IEEE 802.11i implementations in this publication.

This section is intended to provide a high-level overview of IEEE 802.11 security concepts; subsequent sections of the guide discuss individual concepts in much greater depth. Readers who are already familiar with IEEE 802.11 security and the basic additions of IEEE 802.11i might wish to skip this section.

3.1 WLAN Security Concerns

Like other wireless technologies, WLANs typically need to support several security objectives. This is intended to be accomplished through a combination of security features built into the wireless networking standard. The most common security objectives for WLANs are as follows:

- **Confidentiality**—ensure that communication cannot be read by unauthorized parties

- **Integrity**—detect any intentional or unintentional changes to data that occur in transit

- **Availability**—ensure that devices and individuals can access a network and its resources whenever needed

- **Access Control**—restrict the rights of devices or individuals to access a network or resources within a network.

The security objectives for wireless and wired LANs are the same, as are the major high-level categories of threats that they face. Table 3-1 provides a list of the main categories of threats against LANs.

Most WLAN threats typically involve an attacker with access to the radio link between a STA and an AP or between two STAs. Several of the threats listed in Table 3-1 rely on an attacker's ability to intercept and inject network communications. This highlights the most significant difference between protecting wireless and wired LANs: the relative ease of intercepting network communications and inserting new ones from what can only be presumed as the authentic source. In a wired LAN, an attacker would have to

---

[14]   NIST SP 800-48 is available at http://csrc nist gov/publications/nistpubs/800-48/NIST_SP_800-48 pdf

gain physical access to the LAN or remotely compromise systems on the LAN; in a wireless LAN, an attacker simply needs to be within range of the WLAN infrastructure. In addition, an attacker can have the advantage of using highly sensitive directional antennas, which can greatly extend the effective range of the wireless LAN beyond the standardized range.

Table 3-1. Major Threats against LAN Security

Threat Category	Description
Denial of Service	Attacker prevents or prohibits the normal use or management of networks or network devices.
Eavesdropping	Attacker passively monitors network communications for data, including authentication credentials.
Man-in-the-Middle	Attacker actively intercepts the path of communications between two legitimate parties, thereby obtaining authentication credentials and data. Attacker can then masquerade as a legitimate party. In the context of a WLAN, a man-in-the-middle attack can be achieved through a *bogus* or *rogue AP*, which looks like an authorized AP to legitimate parties.
Masquerading	Attacker impersonates an authorized user and gains certain unauthorized privileges.
Message Modification	Attacker alters a legitimate message by deleting, adding to, changing, or reordering it.
Message Replay	Attacker passively monitors transmissions and retransmits messages, acting as if the attacker were a legitimate user.
Traffic Analysis	Attacker passively monitors transmissions to identify communication patterns and participants.

3.2 History of Pre-RSN IEEE 802.11 Security

Prior to the IEEE 802.11i amendment and its RSN framework, IEEE 802.11 had a number of serious security weaknesses.[15] Many vendors have added proprietary features to their IEEE 802.11 implementations to compensate for security flaws in the standard, but proprietary features often prevent interoperability. This section explains pre-RSN security features and shortcomings as a basis for understanding the motivation behind RSN. Sections 3.2.1 through 3.2.5 discuss pre-RSN IEEE 802.11 access control and authentication, encryption, data integrity, replay protection, and availability, respectively.

3.2.1 Access Control and Authentication

The original IEEE 802.11 specification defines two means to validate the identities of wireless devices attempting to gain access to a WLAN, open system authentication and shared key authentication; neither of these alternatives is secure.[16] IEEE 802.11 implementations are required to support open system authentication; shared key authentication support is optional. Open system authentication is effectively a null authentication mechanism that does not provide true identity verification. In practice, a STA is authenticated to an AP simply by providing the following information:

---

[15] Also, many pre-RSN IEEE 802 11 products have security features disabled by default, so they provide little or no protection for wireless communication until they are reconfigured

[16] The shared key authentication scheme based on a unilateral challenge-response mechanism is typically referred to as WEP because it uses the WEP encryption for response computation However, shared key authentication is actually a simple authentication scheme independent of WEP Also, it does not work WEP encrypts the response by XORing the challenge with a pseudo-random key stream generated using a WEP key The attacker can XOR the challenge and the response to expose the key stream, which can subsequently be used to authenticate

■ **Service Set Identifier (SSID) for the AP.** The *SSID* is a name assigned to a WLAN; it allows STAs to distinguish one WLAN from another. SSIDs are broadcast in plaintext in wireless communications, so an eavesdropper can easily learn the SSID for a WLAN. However, the SSID is not an access control feature, and was never intended to be used for that purpose.

■ **Media Access Control (MAC) address for the STA.** A *MAC address* is a (hopefully) unique 48-bit value that is permanently assigned to a particular wireless network interface. Many implementations of IEEE 802.11 allow administrators to specify a list of authorized MAC addresses; the AP will permit devices with those MAC addresses only to use the WLAN. This is known as *MAC address filtering*. However, since the MAC address is not encrypted, it is simple to intercept traffic and identify MAC addresses that are allowed past the MAC filter. Unfortunately, almost all WLAN adapters allow applications to set the MAC address, so it is relatively trivial to spoof a MAC address, meaning attackers can gain unauthorized access easily.

Additionally, the AP is not authenticated to the STA by open system authentication. Therefore, the STA has to trust that it is communicating to the real AP and not an impostor AP that is using the same SSID. Therefore, open system authentication does not provide reasonable assurance of any identities, and can be misused easily to gain unauthorized access to a WLAN or trick users into connecting to a malicious WLAN.

Shared key authentication was supposed to be more robust than open system authentication; in fact, it is equally insecure. As the name implies, shared key authentication is based on a secret cryptographic key known as a Wired Equivalent Privacy (WEP) key; this key is shared by legitimate STAs and APs. (WEP is described in more detail in Section 3.2.2.) Shared key authentication uses a simple challenge-response scheme based on whether the STA seeking WLAN access knows the WEP key. As shown in Figure 3-1, the STA initiates an Authentication Request with the AP, and the AP generates a random 128-bit challenge value and sends it to the STA. Using the WEP key, the STA encrypts the challenge and returns the result to the AP. The AP decrypts the result using the same WEP key and allows the STA access only if the decrypted value is the same as the challenge. The cryptographic computations are performed using the RC4 stream cipher algorithm, which generates a pseudo-random data sequence known as a *key stream*. To encrypt or decrypt data, the key stream is combined with the data.

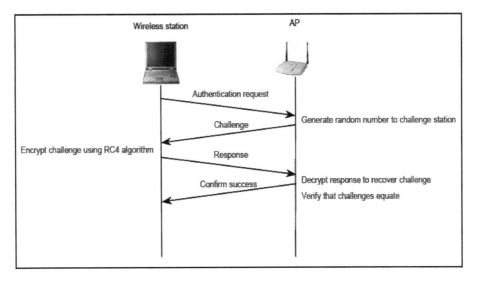

Figure 3-1. Shared Key Authentication Message Flow

Shared key authentication is still weak because the AP is not authenticated to the STA, so there is no assurance that the STA is communicating with a legitimate AP. Also, simple unilateral challenge-response schemes have long been known to be weak unless they are carefully designed, with sufficient entropy in the challenge, keys of the appropriate length, a strong hash function, and secure protocol design. Although the challenge-response messages used for shared key authentication can prevent successful replay of authentication traffic, the challenge-response process can be compromised by methods such as man-in-the-middle attacks and off-line brute force or dictionary attacks.[17]

Additional vulnerabilities in IEEE 802.11's shared key authentication are known and documented. For example, an attacker can eavesdrop, capturing and viewing the cleartext challenge value and the encrypted response. The attacker can then analyze the two pieces of information to determine the WEP key stream. Some organizations prefer using open system authentication because shared key authentication provides so much information to eavesdroppers about the WEP key that it jeopardizes the confidentiality and integrity that should be provided to the communications by the WEP key. Another significant limitation of shared key authentication is that it authenticates the identity of devices but not users. If an attacker gains access to a STA containing a WEP key, the attacker can use that key on any other WEP-capable device to be authenticated and gain access to the WLAN.

Another major problem with shared key authentication is that pre-RSN IEEE 802.11 requires all devices on a WLAN to use the same WEP key or the same small set of keys. This reduces accountability and complicates troubleshooting and incident response efforts. If the WEP key is compromised, it needs to be replaced as quickly as possible to prevent further malicious acts, because WEP keys are used not only for access control, but also to protect confidentiality and integrity (as described in Sections 3.2.2 and 3.2.3). Unfortunately, IEEE 802.11 does not specify any support for key management. When a WEP key needs to be changed, the WLAN administrators have to implement their own methods for generating and distributing a new key. The key needs to be replaced on all STAs and APs, which is a manual process for many WLAN products. WLAN administrators also need to implement methods for archiving, auditing, and destroying keys. Key management problems often limit the scalability of IEEE 802.11 WLANs.

In some cases, shared key authentication is weakened by implementations that use poor WEP keys. For example, some implementations use the WLAN product's default WEP key or set a trivial key, such as all zeroes or all ones. The key should be randomly generated[18] so that it is not easily guessable. This will delay attackers that capture network traffic and perform dictionary attacks against it, hoping to find the key that decrypts the traffic successfully. WEP keys should be changed frequently to reduce the likelihood and impact of any key compromises.

3.2.2 Encryption

The WEP protocol, part of the IEEE 802.11 standard, uses the RC4 stream cipher algorithm to encrypt wireless communications, which protects their contents from disclosure to eavesdroppers. The standard for WEP specifies support for a 40-bit WEP key only; however, many vendors offer non-standard extensions to WEP that support key lengths of up to 128 or even 256 bits. WEP also uses a 24-bit value known as an initialization vector (IV) as a seed value for initializing the cryptographic key stream. For

---

[17] Moreover, the IEEE 802.11 challenge-response scheme does not work properly. WEP encrypts the response by XORing the challenge with a pseudo-random key stream generated using a WEP key. The attacker can XOR the challenge and the response to expose the key stream, which can subsequently be used to authenticate.

[18] For more information about the significance and requirements of random number generation, see RFC 4086, *Randomness Requirements for Security,* found at http://www.ietf.org/rfc/rfc4086.txt. A more technical approach can be found in NIST SP 800-90, *Recommendation for Random Number Generation Using Deterministic Random Bit Generators,* available at http://csrc.nist.gov/publications/nistpubs/800-90/SP800-90_DRBG-June2006-final.pdf

example, a 104-bit WEP key with a 24-bit IV becomes a 128-bit RC4 key. Ideally, larger key sizes translate to stronger protection, but the cryptographic technique used by WEP has known flaws that are not mitigated by longer keys.

Most attacks against WEP encryption have been based on IV-related vulnerabilities. For example, the IV portion of the RC4 key is sent in cleartext, which allows an eavesdropper that monitors and analyzes a relatively small amount of network traffic to recover the key by taking advantage of the IV value knowledge, the relatively small 24-bit IV key space, and a weakness in the way WEP implements the RC4 algorithm. Also, WEP does not specify precisely how the IVs should be set or changed; some products use a static, well-known IV value or reset to zero. If two messages have the same IV, and the plaintext of either message is known, it is relatively trivial for an attacker to determine the plaintext of the second message. In particular, because many messages contain common protocol headers or other easily guessable contents, it is often possible to identify the original plaintext contents with minimal effort. Even traffic from products that use sequentially increasing IV values is still susceptible to attack. There are less than 17 million possible IV values; on a busy WLAN, the entire IV space may be exhausted in a few hours. When the IV is chosen randomly, which represents the best possible generic IV selection algorithm, by the birthday paradox two IVs already have a 50% chance of colliding after about 2^{12} frames.

Another possible threat against confidentiality is network traffic analysis. Eavesdroppers might be able to gain information by monitoring which parties communicate at what times. Also, analyzing traffic patterns can aid in determining the content of communications; for example, short bursts of activity might be caused by terminal emulation or instant messaging, while steady streams of activity might be generated by video conferencing. More sophisticated analysis might be able to determine the operating systems in use based on the length of certain frames. Other than encrypting communications, IEEE 802.11, like most other network protocols, does not offer any features that might thwart network traffic analysis, such as adding random lengths of padding to messages or sending additional messages with randomly generated data.

3.2.3 Data Integrity

WEP performs data integrity checking for messages transmitted between STAs and APs. WEP is designed to reject any messages that have been changed in transit, such as by a man-in-the-middle attack. WEP data integrity is based on a simple encrypted checksum—a 32-bit cyclic redundancy check (CRC-32) computed on each payload prior to transmission. The payload and checksum are encrypted using the RC4 key stream and transmitted. The receiver decrypts them, recomputes the checksum on the received payload, and compares it with the transmitted checksum. If the checksums are not the same, the transmitted data frame has been altered in transit, and the frame is discarded.

Unfortunately, CRC-32 is subject to bit flipping attacks, which means that an attacker knows which CRC-32 bits will change when message bits are altered. WEP attempts to counter this problem by encrypting the CRC-32 to produce an integrity check value (ICV). The creators of WEP believed that an enciphered CRC-32 would be less subject to tampering. However, they did not realize that a property of stream ciphers such as WEP's RC4 is that bit flipping survives the encryption process—the same bits flip whether or not encryption is used. Therefore, the WEP ICV offers no additional protection against bit flipping.

Integrity should be provided by a cryptographic checksum rather than a CRC. Also known as keyed hashes or message authentication codes (MAC), cryptographic checksums prevent bit flipping attacks because they are designed so that any change to the original message results in significant and unpredictable changes to the resulting checksum. CRCs are generally more efficient computationally than cryptographic checksums, but are only designed to protect against random bit errors, not intentional forgeries, so they do not provide the same level of integrity protection.

3.2.4 Replay Protection

The cryptographic implementation provides no protection against replay attacks because it does not include features such as an incrementing counter, timestamp, or other temporal data that would make replayed traffic easily detectable.

3.2.5 Availability

Individuals who do not have physical access to the WLAN infrastructure can cause a denial of service for the WLAN. One threat is known as *jamming,* which involves a device that emits electromagnetic energy on the WLAN's frequencies. The energy makes the frequencies unusable by the WLAN, causing a denial of service. Jamming can be performed intentionally by an attacker or unintentionally by a non-WLAN device transmitting on the same frequency. Another threat against availability is *flooding*, which involves an attacker sending large numbers of messages to an AP at such a high rate that the AP cannot process them, or other STAs cannot access the channel, causing a partial or total denial of service. These threats are difficult to counter in any radio-based communications; thus, the IEEE 802.11 standard does not provide any defense against jamming or flooding. Also, as described in Section 3.2.1, attackers can establish rogue APs; if STAs mistakenly attach to a rogue AP instead of a legitimate one, this could make the legitimate WLAN effectively unavailable to users. Although 802.11i protects data frames, it does not offer protection to control or management frames. An attacker can exploit the fact that management frames are not authenticated to deauthenticate a client or to disassociate a client from the network. [19]

3.3 Brief Overview of IEEE 802.11i Security

The IEEE 802.11i standard is the sixth amendment to the baseline IEEE 802.11 standards. It includes many security enhancements that leverage mature and proven security technologies. For example, IEEE 802.11i references the Extensible Authentication Protocol (EAP) standard, which is a means for providing mutual authentication between STAs and the WLAN infrastructure, as well as performing automatic cryptographic key distribution. Section 6 describes EAP in depth; EAP is a standard developed by the Internet Engineering Task Force (IETF). [20]. IEEE 802.11i employs accepted cryptographic practices, such as generating cryptographic checksums through hash message authentication codes (HMAC).

The IEEE 802.11i specification introduces the concept of a Robust Security Network (RSN). An RSN is defined as a wireless security network that only allows the creation of Robust Security Network Associations (RSNA). An RSNA is a logical connection between communicating IEEE 802.11 entities established through the IEEE 802.11i key management scheme, called the 4-Way Handshake, which is a protocol that validates that both entities share a pairwise master key (PMK), synchronizes the installation of temporal keys, and confirms the selection and configuration of data confidentiality and integrity protocols. The entities obtain the PMK in one of two ways—either the PMK is already configured on each device, in which case it is called a pre-shared key (PSK), or it is distributed as a side effect of a successful EAP authentication instance, which is a component of IEEE 802.1X port-based access control. The PMK serves as the basis for the IEEE 802.11i data confidentiality and integrity protocols that provide

---

[19] The IEEE 802 11w Task Group is working on an extension to 802 11i that will protect some management frames, including disassociation frames

[20] The IETF's Working Groups produce two types of documents: Request for Comment (RFC), which are accepted standards; and Internet-Drafts, which are working documents that may become RFCs The last 2 digits of the name of an Internet-Draft represent its version number (e g , 00 or 05) Since this is subject to change, this document substitutes "xx" for the version number of referenced Internet-Drafts

enhanced security over the flawed WEP. Most large enterprise deployments of RSN technology will use IEEE 802.1X and EAP rather than PSKs because of the difficulty of managing PSKs on numerous devices. WLAN connections employing ad hoc mode, which typically involve only a few STAs, are more likely to use PSKs. The RSN security architecture and RSNAs are discussed in detail in Section 4.

This section provides a brief introduction to the IEEE 802.1X standard, which is specified by the IEEE 802.11i amendment. Two components defined in IEEE 802.1X are relied upon for the establishment of RSNAs: authentication servers and IEEE 802.1X port-based access control. The IEEE 802.1X standard provides a framework for access control that leverages EAP to provide centralized, mutual authentication. IEEE 802.1X was originally developed for wired LANs to prevent unauthorized use in open environments such as university campuses, but it has been used by IEEE 802.11i for WLANs as well. The IEEE 802.1X framework provides the means to block user access until authentication is successful, thereby controlling access to WLAN resources.

The IEEE 802.1X standard defines several terms related to authentication. The *authenticator* is an entity at one end of a point-to-point LAN segment that facilitates authentication of the entity attached to the other end of that link. For example, the AP in Figure 3-2 serves as an authenticator. The *supplicant* is the entity being authenticated. The STA may be viewed as a supplicant.[21] The *authentication server* (AS) is an entity that provides an authentication service to an authenticator. This service determines from the credentials provided by the supplicant whether the supplicant is authorized to access the services provided by the authenticator. The AS provides these authentication services and delivers session keys to each AP in the wireless network; each STA either receives session keys from the AS or derives the session keys itself. The AS either authenticates the STA and AP itself, or provides information to the STA and AP so that they may authenticate each other. The AS typically lies inside the DS, as depicted in Figure 3-2. When employing a solution based on the IEEE 802.11i standard, the AS most often used for authentication is an Authentication, Authorization, and Accounting (AAA) server that uses the Remote Authentication Dial In User Service (RADIUS)[22] or Diameter[23] protocol to transport authentication-related traffic. This is discussed further in Section 4. The supplicant/authenticator model is intrinsically a unilateral rather than mutual authentication model: the supplicant authenticates to the network. IEEE 802.11i combats this bias by requiring that the EAP method used provides mutual authentication.

---

[21] In ad hoc mode, the STA and AP of the IBSS must implement both supplicant and authenticator

[22] *RADIUS* is an IP-based protocol that facilitates the centralized management of authentication, authorization, and accounting (AAA) data For more information on RADIUS, see RFC 2865, *RADIUS*, at http://www.ietf.org/rfc/rfc2865.txt, and RFC 2869, *RADIUS Extensions*, at http://www.ietf.org/rfc/rfc2869.txt

[23] Diameter is specified in RFC 3588, *Diameter Base Protocol*, available at http://www.ietf.org/rfc/rfc3588.txt Like RADIUS, Diameter provides an AAA framework for applications such as network access

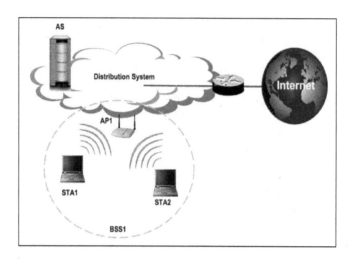

Figure 3-2. Conceptual View of Authentication Server in a Network

Figure 3-3 provides a simple conceptual view of IEEE 802.1X that depicts all the fundamental IEEE 802.11i components: STAs, an AP, and an AS. In this example, the STAs are the supplicants, and the AP is the authenticator. Until successful authentication occurs between a STA and the AS, the STA's communications are blocked by the AP. Because the AP sits at the boundary between the wireless and wired networks, this prevents the unauthenticated STA from reaching the wired network. The technique used to block the communications is known as *port-based access control*. IEEE 802.1X can control data flows by distinguishing between EAP and non-EAP frames, then passing EAP frames through an uncontrolled port and non-EAP frames through a controlled port, which can block access. IEEE 802.11i extends this to block the AP's communication until keys are in place as well. Thus, the IEEE 802.11i extensions prevent a rogue access point from exchanging anything but EAP traffic with the STA's host.

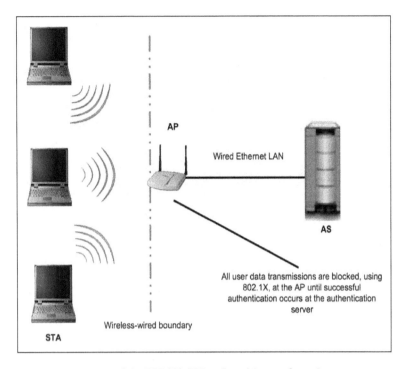

Figure 3-3. IEEE 802.1X Port-Based Access Control

3.4 Summary

Wired and wireless LANs have the same security objectives: confidentiality, integrity, access control, and availability. They also face the same high-level threats: denial of service, eavesdropping, man-in-the-middle, masquerading, message modification, message replay, and traffic analysis. WLAN threats typically involve an attacker with access to the radio link between two STAs or between a STA and an AP. The most significant difference between protecting wireless and wired LANs is the relative ease of intercepting and injecting network communications.

Pre-RSN IEEE 802.11 offers various features intended to provide security; unfortunately, these features contain serious known vulnerabilities that can be exploited to impair access control and authentication, encryption, data integrity checking, and availability. Examples include the following:

- **Access Control and Authentication.** Pre-RSN IEEE 802.11 performs access control through either open system or shared key authentication. Open system authentication does not verify any claimed credentials from the STA, so it is generally suitable only for providing public access to a WLAN. Shared key authentication uses a challenge-response scheme, but it has weaknesses that can permit man-in-the-middle attacks and other compromises. Also, neither open system nor shared key authentication allows a STA to verify the identity of an AP, so attackers can set up rogue APs and trick STAs into using them, potentially impacting confidentiality, integrity, and availability.

- **Encryption.** WEP suffers from a number of cryptographic weaknesses that enable attackers with readily available software tools to decipher captured data, sometimes with as little as a few minutes of recorded traffic. The weaknesses are a result of the way WEP employs the RC4 encryption algorithm and the use of a 24-bit IV, which is too small to prevent recurring IVs on a busy WLAN.

■ **Data Integrity.** WEP attempts to perform data integrity checking for messages and reject messages that have been changed in transit. WEP uses a simple non-cryptographic checksum to detect errors in data transmission and protects this checksum with a stream cipher. Unfortunately, stream ciphers offer no protection against bit-flipping attacks, which means that in many cases a determined adversary can alter both data and the corresponding checksums without detection.

■ **Availability.** Individuals without physical access to the WLAN can impact its availability through two types of attacks: jamming and flooding. Jamming occurs when a device emits electromagnetic energy on the WLAN's frequency, making it unusable. Flooding involves an attacker sending large numbers of messages to an AP at a high rate to prevent the AP from processing traffic. The IEEE 802.11 standard offers no defense against jamming or flooding. Also, attackers can establish rogue APs, which could make the legitimate WLAN effectively unavailable to users.

The IEEE 802.11i specification introduces the concept of an RSN, which is a wireless network that allows the creation of RSNAs only. RSNAs are logical connections between communicating IEEE 802.11 entities established through the IEEE 802.11i 4-Way Handshake. RSNAs allow for the protection of data frames and provide enhanced security relative to the flawed WEP. The IEEE 802.1X framework specified by the IEEE 802.11i amendment provides the means to block user access until authentication is successful, thereby controlling access to the WLAN resources. The technique used to block access is known as port-based access control; it involves the AP distinguishing between EAP and non-EAP frames, then passing EAP frames through an uncontrolled port and non-EAP frames through a controlled port, which can block access.

The IEEE 802.1X standard defines several terms related to authentication: authenticator, supplicant, and authentication server. The authenticator is an entity such as an AP that facilitates an authentication attempt. The supplicant is an entity such as a STA that is authenticated by an authenticator. The authentication server (AS) is an entity that provides an authentication service to an authenticator. This service determines, from the credentials provided by the supplicant, whether the supplicant is authorized to access the services provided by the authenticator. The AS either authenticates the STA and AP itself, or it provides information to the STA and AP so that they may authenticate each other.

4. Security Framework for Robust Security Networks

The IEEE 802.11i amendment allows for enhanced security features beyond WEP and the simple IEEE 802.11 shared key challenge-response authentication. The amendment introduces the concepts of Robust Security Networks (RSN) and Robust Security Network Associations (RSNA). This section explains these terms and describes e security framework for RSN. It also discusses the reasons for creating RSNs. It then explains what constitutes an RSN and an RSNA. The section discusses the cryptographic key hierarchies that relate keys and introduce the alternatives for key distribution. Finally, it describes the two RSN data confidentiality and integrity protocols defined in IEEE 802.11i—Temporal Key Integrity Protocol (TKIP) and Counter Mode with Cipher Block Chaining Message Authentication Code Protocol (CCMP)—and their security features.

This section contains considerable detail on the internal operations of IEEE 802.11 WLANs. It includes detailed descriptions of encryption and decryption procedures, IEEE 802.11 network element message flows, and various protocols. Readers without a need for this technical detail might wish to skim or skip portions of this section, and then read the summary in Section 4.4 carefully.

4.1 Features of RSNs

With the addition of the IEEE 802.11i amendment in 2004, IEEE 802.11 offers two general classes of security capabilities for IEEE 802.11 WLANs. The first class, pre-RSN security, includes the legacy security capabilities developed in the original IEEE 802.11 specification: open system or shared key authentication for validating the identity of a wireless station, and WEP for the confidentiality protection of traffic. The second class of security capabilities includes a number of security mechanisms to create RSNs. An RSN includes security enhancements to address all the known flaws of WEP and provide robust protection for the wireless link, including data integrity and confidentiality. Figure 4-1 provides a high-level taxonomy of the major pre-RSN and RSN security mechanisms.

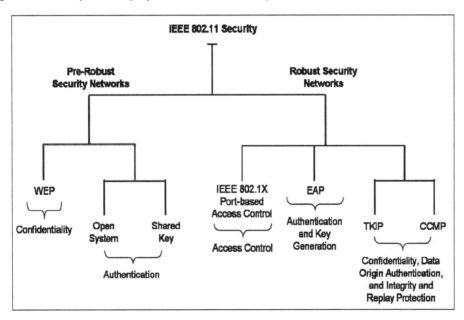

Figure 4-1. Taxonomy for Pre-RSN and RSN Security

At a high level, RSN includes IEEE 802.1X port-based access control, key management techniques, and the TKIP and CCMP data confidentiality and integrity protocols. Described in Section 4.3, these protocols allow for the creation of several diverse types of security networks because of the numerous configuration options. RSN security is at the link level only,[24] providing protection for traffic between a wireless STA and its associated AP, or between one wireless STA and another wireless STA. It does not provide end-to-end application-level security, such as between a STA and an e-mail or Web server on the DS, because communication between these entities requires more than just one link. To provide end-to-end security, organizations can implement network level security mechanisms such as Transport Layer Security (TLS) or IPsec. Also, RSN's security features apply only to the wireless portion of the overall network, not to communications on wired networks. As shown in Figure 4-2, the security provided in an RSN can apply to both IEEE 802.11 modes of operation, BSS (infrastructure mode) and IBSS (ad hoc mode).[25] For infrastructure mode, additional measures need to be taken to provide end-to-end security.

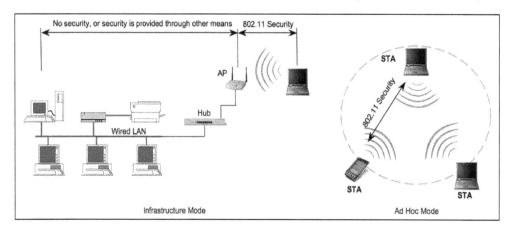

Figure 4-2. Security in Ad Hoc and Infrastructure Modes

The IEEE 802.11i amendment defines an *RSN* as a wireless network that allows the creation of RSN Associations (RSNA) only. An *RSNA* is a security relationship established by the IEEE 802.11i 4-Way Handshake, which is described in Section 5.5. The 4-Way Handshake validates that the parties to the protocol instance both possess a pairwise master key (PMK), synchronizes the installation of temporal keys, and confirms the selection of cipher suites. The PMK is the cornerstone for a number of security features absent from WEP. Complete robust security is considered to be possible only when all devices in the network use RSNAs. In practice, some networks have a mix of RSNAs and non-RSNA connections. A network that allows the creation of both pre-RSN associations (pre-RSNA) and RSNAs is referred to as a *Transition Security Network* (TSN). A TSN is intended to be an interim means to provide connectivity while an organization migrates to networks based exclusively on RSNAs.

---

24   A *link layer protocol* describes the rules for communication between two entities over a particular communications medium, such as air (wireless networking) or various cable types (wired networking) It defines how these entities are uniquely addressed, how the medium will be shared when more than two entities use it simultaneously, and how to correct for errors in transmission Link layer protocols are distinguished from network layer protocols, which focus primarily on routing data packets over multiple links, and perhaps over multiple media types For example, the packets of a network layer protocol such as IP might travel over a number of links from source to destination Different link layer protocols (e g , Point-to-Point Protocol [PPP], IEEE 802 11, IEEE 802 16) might govern the transmission of the IP packets over each of the links

25   Although RSNs may be created for both BSS and IBSS WLANs, this guide only describes the security algorithms and protocols for BSSs Significant differences between these modes are highlighted

RSNAs enable the following security features for IEEE 802.11 WLANs, which are explained thoroughly later in this section and in Section 5:

■ Enhanced user authentication mechanisms

■ Cryptographic key management

■ Data confidentiality

■ Data origin authentication and integrity

■ Replay protection.

An RSNA relies on IEEE 802.1X to provide an authentication framework. To achieve the robust security of RSNAs, the designers of the IEEE 802.11i amendment used numerous mature cryptographic algorithms and techniques (as described in Section 3.3). Figure 4-3 provides a taxonomy of the cryptographic algorithms included in the IEEE 802.11 standard. These algorithms can be categorized as being used for confidentiality, integrity (and data origin authentication), or key generation. All of the algorithms specifically referenced in the IEEE 802.11 standard are symmetric algorithms, which use the same key for two different steps of the algorithm, such as encryption and decryption.

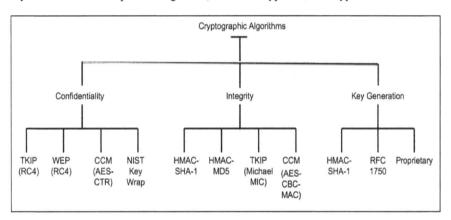

Figure 4-3. Cryptographic Algorithms Used in IEEE 802.11[26]

4.2 Key Hierarchies and Key Distribution and Management

Fundamental to any cryptographic system are the cryptographic keys used in the transformation (enciphering or deciphering) processes. Since cryptography is the security foundation of IEEE 802.11 WLANs, the security of keys is particularly important. NIST's 2-volume guidance document on Key Management, SP 800-57, includes general guidance as well as best practices recommendations. [27] Keys typically need to meet the following requirements:

■ Randomly generated to reduce the probability that they can be determined by an adversary or that they will be reused

---

[26] The IEEE 802 11i amendment specifically references these cryptographic algorithms Other cryptographic algorithms for confidentiality, integrity, or key generation may be incorporated by reference in one of the numerous EAP methods that may be used in a particular implementation These additional cryptographic algorithms have been excluded from this diagram

[27] It can be found at http://csrc nist gov/publications/nistpubs/800-57/SP800-57-Part1 pdf and http://csrc nist gov/publications/nistpubs/800-57/SP800-57-Part2 pdf

- Changed frequently to reduce the possibility of discovery through sophisticated cryptanalysis

- Protected while in storage, so that previous communications cannot be deciphered

- Protected during transmission

- Erased completely when no longer needed.

These requirements are related to the security service known as *key management*, which is defined as "the process of handling and controlling cryptographic keys and related material (such as initialization values) during their life cycle in a cryptographic system, including ordering, generating, distributing, storing, loading, escrowing, archiving, auditing, and destroying the material."[28] The IEEE 802.11 specification provides guidelines for some general key requirements, but it leaves other areas open to interpretation and dependent on implementation. Section 7 provides additional guidance on these requirements.

For pre-RSN IEEE 802.11 networks that used manual WEP keys, key management was non-existent. For instance, there was typically only one key (or a small number of keys) for all devices in the network, and there was no standard mechanism for distributing the keys. Networks using dynamic WEP did have basic key distribution protocols that were able to derive per-user session keys, but still retained all the weaknesses inherent in WEP. However, with RSNAs there are several inter-related keys that underlie the security functions of encryption, authentication, and integrity. IEEE 802.11i defines two key hierarchies for RSNAs that specify the inter-relations of the keys. The two key hierarchies are the Pairwise Key Hierarchy, which is designed for unicast traffic[29] protection, and the Group Key Hierarchy, which is intended for multicast/broadcast traffic[30] protection. Sections 4.2.1 and 4.2.2 describe these key hierarchies and explain the source of each key and the relationships among keys.

4.2.1 Pairwise Key Hierarchy

Figure 4-4 depicts the Pairwise Key Hierarchy. The two keys depicted at the top of the key hierarchy are known as *root keys,* which are used as the basis for generating additional keys required for various confidentiality and integrity protections. The root keys represent the two ways in which keys may be installed in IEEE 802.11 RSNA devices, as follows:

- **Pre-Shared Key (PSK).** A *PSK* is a static key delivered to the AS and the STA through an out-of-band mechanism, as shown in Figure 4-5. The PSK must be put into place before establishing an association. The PSK may be generated and installed in any number of ways, including proprietary automated public-key cryptographic approaches, and manual means such as a USB device or a passphrase (which can be converted to a cryptographic key using one of a number of algorithms). If any of the PSKs are compromised, they must be re-distributed in the same way. The security of the WLAN is compromised if any of the PSKs does not possess sufficient cryptographic strength; the passphrase from which the PSK is generated must be a long and complex, possibly randomly generated. The IEEE 802.11 standard does not specify how PSKs are to be generated or distributed, so these decisions are left to implementers.[31] As a result, organizations should review any PSK approach carefully for possible vulnerabilities and evaluate its performance implications. Distributing PSKs in a large network might be infeasible. Due to client software limitations, a common practice is to assign a single PSK per SSID to enable

---

[28] This definition is from RFC 2828, *Internet Security Glossary*, which is available at http://www.ietf.org/rfc/rfc2828.txt
[29] Unicast data transfer is a one-to-one type of transmission, used for communications between an AP and a particular STA
[30] A multicast data transfer is a one-to-many type of transmission; data is destined for a subset of all the STAs in a WLAN A broadcast data transfer is a one-to-all type of transmission where data is sent to all STAs on a WLAN
[31] Annex H 4 does, however, recommend a passphrase to key conversion scheme that WPA2 certification enforces This scheme uses PKCS 5 and HMAC-SHA1

roaming. In such a case, all users can decrypt the traffic of other users, even if the network is protected from outsiders.

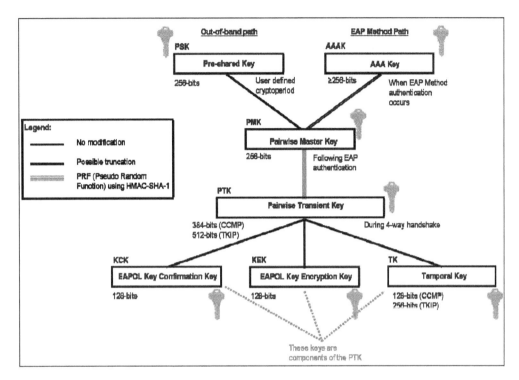

Figure 4-4. Pairwise Key Hierarchy

- **Authentication, Authorization, and Accounting Key (AAAK).** The *AAA key*, also known as the Master Session Key (MSK), is delivered to the AP through the Extensible Authentication Protocol (EAP) during the process of establishing an RSNA. Each time a user[32] authenticates to the WLAN, the AAA key changes; the new key is then used for the duration of the user's session, which lasts until the key lifetime expires or the user reauthenticates. As discussed in Section 5, numerous authentication techniques can be used with EAP. Delivery of the AAA key relies on the key generation capability of the chosen EAP authentication method. All EAP authentication methods supporting IEEE 802.11 RSNs must have the ability to create the AAA key for RSN security features to function properly. Decisions on the appropriate EAP authentication methods are left to the implementers of STAs or the AS. As a result, organizations should carefully review any EAP authentication methods and AAA key generation approaches for possible vulnerabilities.[33]

---

[32] There is a gap between design and practice The IEEE 802 1X model really addresses device authentication Some databases can store device information In many real deployments, however, the mobile device proxies authentication credentials of the current user to allow reuse of the extensive user authentication databases already in place

[33] EAP standardization and vulnerability information can be found on the Web sites of the IETF's EAP Working Group (http://www ietf org/html charters/eap-charter html) and EAP Method Update (emu) Working Group (http://www ietf org/html charters/emu-charter html)

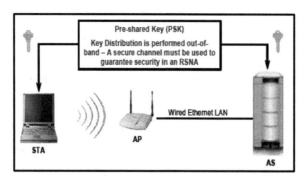

Figure 4-5. Out-of-Band Key Distribution for the PSK

As shown in Figure 4-4, the root key—either the PSK or the AAAK—is used to formulate the Pairwise Master Key (PMK). The *PMK* is a key-generating key used for the derivation of the Pairwise Transient Key (PTK), along with the MAC address of the STA and AP and nonces that each creates for the key generation process. Using the STA and AP addresses in the generation of the PTK provides protection against session hijacking and impersonation; using nonces provides additional random keying material. The *PTK* is composed of the following three keys:

- **EAP Over LAN (EAPOL) Key Confirmation Key (EAPOL-KCK)**, which is used to support the integrity and data origin authenticity of STA-to-AP control frames during operational setup of an RSN.[34] It also performs an access control function: proof-of-possession of the PMK. An entity that possesses the PMK is authorized to use the link.

- **EAPOL Key Encryption Key (EAPOL-KEK)**, which is used to protect the confidentiality of keys and other data during some RSNA procedures.

- **Temporal Key (TK)**, which is used to provide the actual protection for user traffic.

Figure 4-4 shows the bit length of each of these keys. The PSK is 256 bits long, and the AAAK is 256 bits long or greater. The TK has two different sizes depending on the data confidentiality and integrity protocol that is used (128 bits for CCMP, 256 bits for TKIP). This is due to differences in cryptographic approaches. Also shown beneath each key is the condition under which the key is generated. For instance, the PMK is created for each session following the EAP authentication process.

Figure 4-4 also shows the *Pseudo-Random Function* (PRF), which is an algorithm that is used to generate the PTK from the PMK. It uses HMAC-SHA-1[35] with specific inputs: the PMK, two 256-bit nonces,[36] and the addresses of the STA and AP. The PRF may be used in IEEE 802.11 for the generation of keys of bit lengths 128, 192, 256, 384 and 512.

---

[34] EAPOL is discussed in Section 5
[35] HMAC is defined in RFC 2104, *HMAC: Keyed-Hashing for Message Authentication* (http://www.ietf.org/rfc/rfc2104.txt)
  SHA-1 is defined by FIPS PUB 180-2 (http://csrc.nist.gov/publications/fips/fips180-2/fips180-2withchangenotice.pdf)
[36] A *nonce* is a non-repeating or random number that is used by a message exchange protocol for detecting replay attacks

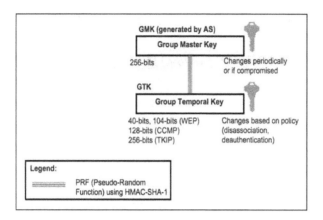

Figure 4-6. Group Key Hierarchy

4.2.2 Group Key Hierarchy

The second key hierarchy defined by IEEE 802.11 is the Group Key Hierarchy, which is depicted in Figure 4-6 and consists of a single key, the Group Temporal Key (GTK). Unlike the PMK, which is generated using material from both supplicant and authenticator, the GTK is generated by the authenticator (AP) and transmitted to its associated STAs. Exactly how this GTK is generated is undefined and is likely to vary considerably in various vendor implementations, with possible implications for security. IEEE 802.11i, however, requires that its value is computationally indistinguishable from random.

The GTK is a 256-bit value for TKIP, 128 bit value for CCMP, and 40- or 104-bit value for WEP. Figure 4-6 also shows the time or condition under which each key is changed.

Table 4-1 presents all of the keys used in IEEE 802.11, as introduced by the IEEE 802.11i amendment.

4.3 Overview of RSN Data Confidentiality and Integrity Protocols

The IEEE 802.11i amendment defines two RSNA data confidentiality and integrity protocols: Temporal Key Integrity Protocol (TKIP) and Counter Mode with Cipher Block Chaining MAC Protocol (CCMP). According to its designers, TKIP was created to allow already-deployed devices to address the numerous inadequacies of WEP. TKIP may be implemented through software updates; it does not require hardware replacement of AP and STAs. However, because TKIP uses RC4 and the Michael message integrity code (MIC) (described in Section 4.3.1.2), both of which have known weaknesses, TKIP is not suitable for high assurance environments. For these environments, CCMP is considered the better solution. However, CCMP requires computing resources that cannot be assumed on pre-RSN hardware. In nearly all cases, organizations seeking to deploy IEEE 802.11 RSNs based on CCMP will need to replace some of their existing IEEE 802.11 equipment.[37] Support for CCMP is mandatory for any device claiming RSNA compliance, while TKIP support is optional. TKIP and CCMP are described further in Sections 4.3.1 and 4.3.2, respectively.

---

[37] A software upgrade to support CCMP is possible on most laptops, but not on most PDAs and APs

Table 4-1. Summary of Keys Used for Data Confidentiality and Integrity Protocols

Abbre-viation	Name	Description / Purpose	Size (bits)	Type
AAA Key	Authentication, Accounting, and Authorization Key	Used to derive the PMK. Used with the IEEE 802.1X authentication and key management approach. Same as MSK.	≥ 256	Key generation key, root key
PSK	Pre-Shared Key	Becomes the PMK in pre-shared key environments.	256	Key generation key, root key
PMK	Pairwise Master Key	Used with other inputs to derive the PTK.	256	Key generation key
GMK	Group Master Key	Used with other inputs to derive the GTK.	128	Key generation key
PTK	Pairwise Transient Key	Derived from the PMK. Comprises the EAPOL-KCK, EAPOL-KEK, and TK and (for TKIP) the MIC key.	512 (TKIP) 384 (CCMP)	Composite key
TK	Temporal Key	Used with TKIP or CCMP to provide confidentiality and integrity protection for unicast user traffic.	256 (TKIP) 128 (CCMP)	Traffic key
GTK	Group Temporal Key	Derived from the GMK. Used to provide confidentiality and integrity protection for multicast/broadcast user traffic.	256 (TKIP) 128 (CCMP) 40, 104 (WEP)	Traffic key
MIC Key	Message Integrity Code Key	Used by TKIP's Michael MIC to provide integrity protection of messages.	64	Message integrity key
EAPOL-KCK	EAPOL-Key Confirmation Key	Used to provide integrity protection for key material distributed during the 4-Way Handshake.	128	Message integrity key
EAPOL-KEK	EAPOL-Key Encryption Key	Used to ensure the confidentiality of the GTK and other key material in the 4-Way Handshake.	128	Traffic key / key encryption key
WEP Key	Wired Equivalent Privacy Key	Used with WEP.	40, 104	Traffic key

4.3.1 Temporal Key Integrity Protocol (TKIP)

TKIP is a cipher suite for enhancing the WEP protocol on pre-RSN hardware without causing significant performance degradation. TKIP works within the processing constraints of first-generation STAs and APs, and therefore enables increased security without requiring hardware replacement. This section provides an overview of TKIP, lists TKIP security features, and briefly describes the TKIP encapsulation and decapsulation procedures, as well as the additional countermeasures that are available.

TKIP provides the following fundamental security features for IEEE 802.11 WLANs:

- Confidentiality protection using the RC4 algorithm[38]

- Integrity protection against several types of attacks[39] using the Michael message digest algorithm (through generation of a message integrity code [MIC])[40]

---

[38] RC4 does not meet FIPS requirements for cryptographic algorithms Accordingly, Federal agencies and others requiring FIPS-validated solutions cannot use WLAN security solutions based on RC4, including both TKIP and WEP
[39] These attacks include modifying the destination address in bit flipping attacks, fragmentation attacks, and iterative key guessing attacks; and modifying the source address in impersonation attacks

- Replay prevention through a frame sequencing technique

- Use of a new encryption key for each frame to prevent attacks such as the Fluhrer-Mantin-Shamir (FMS) attack, which can compromise WEP-based WLANs[41]

- Implementation of countermeasures whenever the STA or AP encounters a frame with a MIC error, which is a strong indication of an active attack.

Sections 4.3.1.1 and 4.3.1.2 briefly describe the TKIP encapsulation and decapsulation procedures, including countermeasures.

4.3.1.1 TKIP Encapsulation

Encapsulation is the process of generating the cryptographic payload (ciphertext) from the plaintext data. The plaintext data comprises user traffic and the source and destination MAC addresses. TKIP encapsulation builds upon the WEP encapsulation technique, modifying WEP with additional features through software, to bolster security without requiring hardware changes. TKIP uses three distinct keys: two integrity keys and an encryption key. The primary characteristics of TKIP encapsulation are presented briefly as follows:

- Two 64-bit message integrity keys are used with the Michael message digest algorithm to produce a message integrity code (MIC). One key is used to provide integrity protection for each half-duplex data channel between the STA and AP. The MIC is computed over the user data, source and destination addresses, and priority bits to provide data integrity. Due to design constraints, an attacker can use sophisticated methods to forge information without detection. Accordingly, TKIP decapsulation employs additional countermeasures, as discussed in Section 4.3.1.2, to partially mitigate the risk of these attacks.

- A monotonically increasing TKIP Sequence Counter (TSC) is assigned to each frame. The TSC provides protection against replay attacks. If frames do not arrive in order, the receiver simply drops them.

- A two-phase cryptographic key-mixing process occurs to produce a new key for every frame that is transmitted. The process takes a session Temporal Key along with the dynamically changing TSC to create a dynamic WEP key.

- The original user frame, the computed 64-bit MIC, and the transmitter address are encrypted using WEP (with RC4) and the per-frame WEP key. Dynamic key updates and other countermeasures provide additional security.

Although the destination and source addresses and priority and payload are used as inputs by the Michael algorithm, only the payload is encrypted. Because the frame header contains the source and destination addresses and priority, the MIC generated by Michael incorporates them. This prevents an adversary from modifying the frame header addresses to spoof the source or redirect the frame to an unauthorized

---

[40] For more information on Michael and its MIC, see Niels Ferguson's 2002 paper, "Michael: An Improved MIC for 802 11 WEP", at http://grouper ieee org/groups/802/11/Documents/DocumentHolder/2-020 zip

[41] Developed in 2001, the FMS attack is now codified in tools that can crack WEP with a few hours of recorded traffic A full explanation of the attack is beyond the scope of this document However, it relies on the fact that certain weak IVs can generate predictable key streams The attack also leverages the fact that protocols limit the possible options for frame and packet headers, even if they are encrypted prior to transmission With known ciphertext and good guesses available for both the key stream and portions of the plaintext, the FMS technique can discover the underlying WEP key Because the FMS attack iteratively uncovers the key one byte at a time, increasing the length of the key is a futile defense against the attack

destination. The TKIP encapsulation process also involves encrypting the MIC using WEP, which helps to hide information about the 64-bit MIC key.

4.3.1.2 TKIP Decapsulation and Countermeasures

Decapsulation is the process to recover the content of protected frames—that is, to decrypt a received ciphertext packet. During decapsulation, various checks are performed on the frames. For example, if the TSC indicates a violation of proper frame sequencing (it should be monotonically increasing), the frame is discarded. Also, the MIC is recomputed and compared with the MIC in the packet; if they do not match, the frame is discarded and TKIP countermeasures are invoked, which serve as a TKIP safety net.

Although the Michael MIC offers increased message integrity protection in comparison with the legacy WEP and its use of an encrypted CRC, Michael is much weaker than what is usually required. Its objective is to provide reasonable levels of integrity assurance on pre-RSNA-compliant devices without requiring hardware upgrades. Michael is subject to a 2^{29} differential cryptanalysis attack, meaning an attacker could expect to create a forgery in about 2^{28} messages on average. Since the Michael MIC has known vulnerabilities, any failure of the message integrity check in TKIP represents a probable active attack. Therefore, TKIP employs additional countermeasures to help thwart these attacks. These countermeasures accomplish the following security goals:[42]

- **Logging security events.** MIC failures during decapsulation at the STA or AP likely mean an active attack. These are to be logged, and a system or security administrator should investigate.

- **Limiting MIC failures.** A receiving STA or AP that detects two failures within a 60-second period disables reception for 60 seconds, not allowing any new associations for STAs using TKIP. This suspense mechanism thwarts an adversary's attempts at numerous attacks in a short period, limiting what an active attacker can learn about any Michael key. The countermeasures effectively limit the adversary to random guessing attacks.

- **Changing the PTK and GTK.** Temporal keys are erased and must be re-initialized.

- **Blocking the IEEE 802.1X ports.** If IEEE 802.1X authentication is used, the state machine is initialized, thereby blocking the controlled ports.

4.3.2 Counter Mode with Cipher Block Chaining MAC Protocol (CCMP)

CCMP is the second data confidentiality and integrity protocol that may be negotiated as a cipher suite for the protection of user traffic in an RSNA. Like TKIP, CCMP was developed to address all known inadequacies of WEP; however, CCMP was developed without the constraint of requiring the use of existing hardware. CCMP is considered the long-term solution for the creation of RSNs for WLANs. It is mandatory for RSN compliance.

CCMP is based on CCM, a generic authenticated encryption block cipher mode of AES.[43] CCM is a mode of operation defined for any block cipher with a 128-bit block size. CCM combines two well-known and proven cryptographic techniques to achieve robust security. First, CCM uses CTR for confidentiality and Cipher Block Chaining MAC (CBC-MAC) for both authentication and integrity protection. CCMP protects the integrity of both the packet data and portions of the IEEE 802.11 header. CCM for IEEE 802.11 employs a single 128-bit session key (TK) to protect the duplex data channel. The

---

[42] The existence of the countermeasures, which include temporary termination of service, enables an attacker to perform a denial of service attack by generating MIC errors In this case, TKIP preserves integrity at the expense of availability

[43] CCM is defined by RFC 3610, *Counter with CBC-MAC (CCM)* (http://www.ietf.org/rfc/rfc3610.txt) AES is defined by FIPS PUB 197 (http://csrc.nist.gov/publications/fips/fips197/fips-197.pdf)

CCMP key space has size 2^{128} and uses a 48-bit packet number (PN) to construct a nonce to prevent replay attacks. The construction of the nonce allows the key to be used for both integrity and confidentiality without compromising either.[44]

As the long-term IEEE 802.11 WLAN solution for confidentiality and integrity, CCMP uses CCM, which was specifically designed to possess the following characteristics:

- A single cryptographic key for confidentiality and integrity to minimize complexity and maximize performance (minimize key scheduling time)[45]

- Integrity protection of the packet header and packet payload, in addition to providing confidentiality of the payload

- Computation of some cryptographic parameters prior to the receipt of packets to enable fast comparisons when they arrive, which reduces latency

- Small footprint (hardware or software implementation size) to minimize costs

- Small security-related packet overhead (minimal data expansion due to cryptographic padding and integrity field, for instance)

- No encumbrance by any existing or pending patents.

Sections 4.3.2.1 and 4.3.2.2 briefly describe the CCMP encapsulation and decapsulation procedures.

4.3.2.1 CCMP Encapsulation

CCMP encapsulation is the process of generating the cryptographic payload (ciphertext) from the plaintext data. The plaintext data comprises user traffic and a MAC header. The primary steps of CCMP encapsulation are the following:

- The packet number (PN) maintained for the session is incremented.

- The PN and other portions of the address field are combined to form the nonce.

- The identifier for the Temporal Key, or KeyID, and the PN are combined to form the CCMP header.

- The frame header is used to construct the Additional Authentication Data (AAD). The AAD is a 22-byte or 28-byte parameter comprising several fields, including several addresses and the quality-of-service control field, that are used as additional input into the CCM authentication process.

- The AAD, nonce, and plaintext data are provided as inputs to CCM along with the Temporal Key to encrypt the data.

- The packet header, the CCM header, and the ciphertext data are concatenated to form the ciphertext (or encapsulated) packet

---

[44] See Jakob Jonsson's paper (http://csrc.nist.gov/CryptoToolkit/modes/proposedmodes/ccm/ccm-ad1.pdf) for the proof of security in the standard model

[45] The design goal was to minimize state on constrained systems

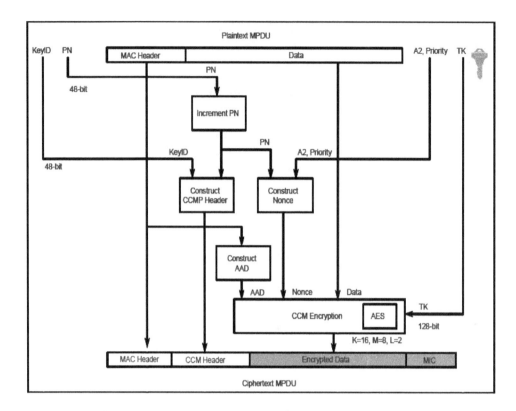

Figure 4-7. CCMP Encapsulation Block Diagram

CCM is an "authenticate-and-encrypt" block cipher mode of AES. As such, it both encrypts and produces a MIC. As shown, the four inputs to the CCM processing are the following:

- 128-bit cryptographic key, TK

- 48-bit nonce (derived for a 48-bit packet number, PN)

- Additional Authentication Data (AAD)

- Variable length packet (frame body) with header.

CCM uses a new Temporal Key every session—with every new STA-AP association. Unlike TKIP, the use of AES at the core of CCM obviates the need to have per-packet keys. As a result, the two-phase key mixing functions of TKIP encapsulation are not present in the CCMP encapsulation. Figure 4-7 depicts the CCMP encapsulation. This illustrates the various functions and their sequence in the encapsulation process.

The figure depicts the plaintext frame prior to transmission at the top, and the plaintext header and ciphertext output at the bottom, ready to send. The payload is transformed into encrypted data along with the integral MIC. For IEEE 802.11 WLANs, the length of the MIC is set to 8 bytes, shown as M=8 in the figure. The K=16 and L=2 denote the 16-byte AES key size and 2-byte maximum packet length field, respectively. Also, CCMP uses the 48-bit packet number as an IV. The increment PN function ensures that the packet number is new for every frame that is encrypted. The 48-bit packet number, which

4-12

provides replay prevention, ensures that the lifetime of an AES key (the per session temporal key, TK) is longer than any possible STA-AP association.

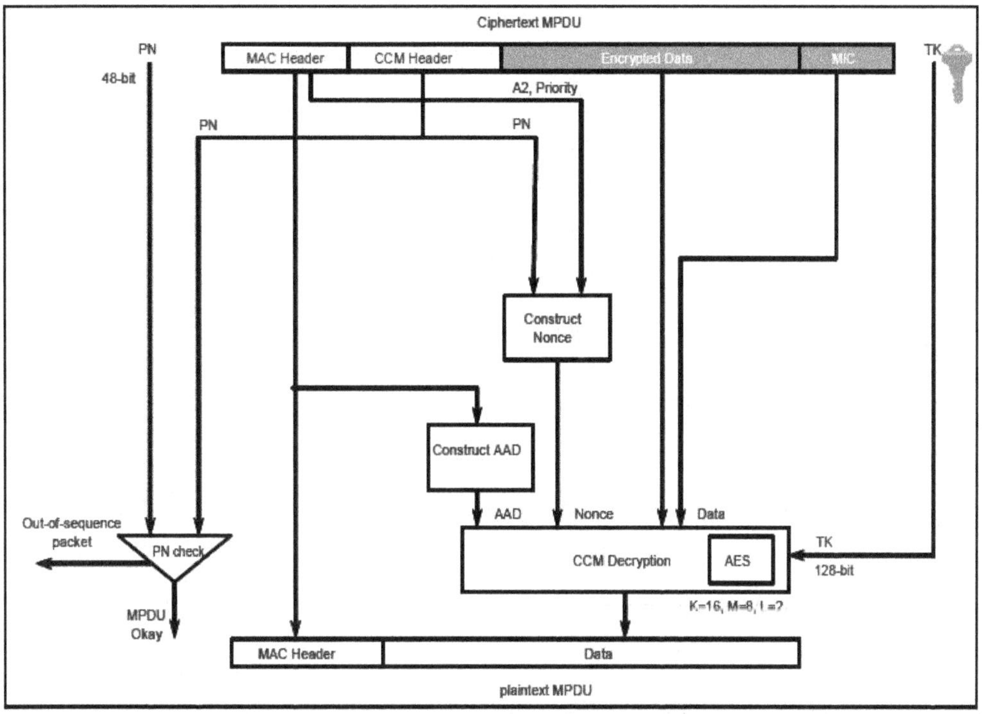

Figure 4-8. CCMP Decapsulation Block Diagram

4.3.2.2 CCMP Decapsulation and Processing

CCMP decapsulation is used to recover and decrypt a transmitted frame. The key steps of CCMP decapsulation are depicted in Figure 4-8 and summarized briefly as follows:

1. The encrypted frame is parsed to re-construct the AAD and the nonce. The AAD is formed from the frame header.

2. The nonce is formed from the PN plus the A2 (transmit address) and Priority fields.

3. CCM uses the Temporal key, AAD, nonce, MIC, and encrypted payload to recover the plaintext data and to verify the MIC. If the MIC integrity check fails, CCM will not return the plaintext.

4. The received frame header and the plaintext data are concatenated to form the plaintext frame.

5. The PN in the frame is validated against the PN maintained for the session. If the PN received is not greater than the session PN, the frame is simply discarded; this check prevents replay attacks.

4.4 Summary

An RSN is a wireless network that only allows the creation of RSNAs. An RSNA is a security relationship based on the IEEE 802.11i 4-Way Handshake that allows for the protection of data frames and provides enhanced security over the now-antiquated WEP. RSNAs enable the following security features for IEEE 802.11 WLANs:

- Enhanced user authentication mechanisms

- Cryptographic key management

- Data confidentiality

- Data origin authentication and integrity

- Replay protection.

RSNAs use several cryptographic keys to support key derivation, encryption, authentication, and integrity functions. The IEEE 802.11i specification defines two key hierarchies for RSNAs: the Pairwise Key Hierarchy, which is designed for unicast traffic protection, and the Group Key Hierarchy, which is intended for multicast/broadcast traffic protection. In the Pairwise Key Hierarchy, there are two ways in which keys may be installed in RSNA devices, as follows:

- **Pre-Shared Key (PSK),** which is a static key delivered to the AS and the STA through an out-of-band mechanism. The IEEE 802.11 standard does not specify how PSKs are to be generated or distributed, so these decisions are left to implementers. The security of the WLAN is compromised if any of the PSKs does not possess sufficient cryptographic strength. As a result, organizations should review any PSK approach carefully for possible vulnerabilities and evaluate its performance implications. Distributing PSKs in a large network might be infeasible.

- **Authentication, Authorization, and Accounting (AAA) Key (AAAK),** also known as the Master Session Key (MSK), which is delivered to the AP through the Extensible Authentication Protocol (EAP) during the process of establishing an RSNA. Each time a user authenticates to the WLAN, the AAA key changes; the new key is then used for the duration of the user's session. Decisions on the appropriate EAP authentication methods are left to the implementers of STAs or the AS. As a result, organizations should carefully review any EAP authentication methods and AAA key generation approaches for possible vulnerabilities.

The IEEE 802.11i amendment defines the following two data confidentiality and integrity protocols for providing confidentiality and integrity for RSNAs:

- **Temporal Key Integrity Protocol (TKIP).** TKIP is intended as an interim solution for IEEE 802.11 WLANs to address the numerous inadequacies of WEP expeditiously. TKIP may be implemented through software updates; it does not require hardware replacement of APs and STAs.

- **Counter Mode with Cipher Block Chaining Message Authentication Code Protocol (CCMP).** CCMP is considered the long-term solution for IEEE 802.11 WLANs. CCMP requires hardware updates and will require that organizations replace their pre-RSN IEEE 802.11 equipment.

Table 4-2 compares the security features of WEP, TKIP, and CCMP. Support for CCMP is mandatory for any device claiming RSNA compliance. As indicated in the table, only CCMP uses a core cryptographic algorithm that is FIPS-compliant. For other security features, CCMP offers the same or stronger implementations than WEP and TKIP. Accordingly, NIST requires the use of CCMP for Federal agencies. For legacy IEEE 802.11 equipment that does not provide CCMP, auxiliary security protection is required; one possibility is the use of an IPsec VPN, using FIPS-approved cryptographic algorithms. NIST SP 800-48 contains specific recommendations for securing legacy IEEE 802.11 implementations.[46]

Table 4-2. Summary of Data Confidentiality and Integrity Protocols

Security Feature	Manual WEP (pre-RSN)	Dynamic WEP (pre-RSN)	TKIP (RSN)	CCMP (RSN)
Core cryptographic algorithm	RC4	RC4	RC4	AES
Key sizes	40-bit or 104-bit (encryption)	40-bit or 104-bit (encryption)	128-bit (encryption), 64-bit (integrity protection)	128-bit (encryption and integrity protection)
Per-packet key	Created through concatenation of WEP key and the 24-bit IV	Derived from EAP authentication	Created through TKIP mixing function	Not needed; temporal key is sufficiently secure
Integrity mechanism	Enciphered CRC-32	Enciphered CRC-32	Michael MIC with countermeasures	CCM
Header protection	None	None	Source and destination addresses protected by Michael MIC	Source and destination addresses protected by CCM
Replay detection	None	None	Enforce IV sequencing	Enforce IV sequencing
Authentication	Open system or shared key	EAP method with IEEE 802.1X	EAP method with IEEE 802.1X or PSK	EAP method with IEEE 802.1X or PSK
Key distribution	Manual	IEEE 802.1X	IEEE 802.1X or manual	IEEE 802.1X or manual

---

[46] NIST SP 800-48 is available at http://csrc.nist.gov/publications/nistpubs/800-48/NIST_SP_800-48.pdf

This page has been left blank intentionally.

5. Robust Security Networks Principles of Operation

This section describes the general principles of operation for IEEE 802.11 RSNs. Section 5.1 begins by describing the flow of frames in establishing an association. The rest of Section 5.1 discusses the types of IEEE 802.11 frames used within an RSN, including the structure of data frames. Section 5.2 provides a high-level overview of the five phases of RSN operation, while Sections 5.3 through 5.7 provide detailed descriptions of each phase. Readers who are looking for only an overview of IEEE 802.11 RSN operation without extensive technical details should read the beginning of Section 5.1 and all of Section 5.2, skim the rest of Section 5, and read the summary in Section 5.8.

5.1   General Principles of IEEE 802.11 Operation

The IEEE 802.11 media access control (MAC) protocol supplies the functionality in WLANs that is required to provide reliable delivery of user data over the potentially noisy, unreliable wireless media. The IEEE 802.11 MAC protocol implements a frame exchange protocol in which the STA receiving a frame either returns an acknowledgement to the frame's source that the frame was received correctly, or notifies the source of an error. The frame exchange protocol is executed by each STA in the WLAN; every STA receives, decodes, and responds to information in the MAC header for every frame that it receives, with the exception of certain broadcast, multicast, and beacon frames.

Figure 5-1 depicts a typical two-frame flow for IEEE 802.11 WLAN communication that illustrates an Association Request and Response. First, the STA sends an Association Request frame to the AP, which is a request to connect to the WLAN with a Service Set Identifier (SSID) of "NotSecure". The *SSID* is a text name assigned to the WLAN. The AP with the matching SSID then responds to the STA with either success or failure. If the response indicates success, the result is an association (not yet an RSNA) between the AP and STA. Association is a record-keeping procedure that allows the DS to keep track of STA location, so that frames from the DS are forwarded to the correct STAs.

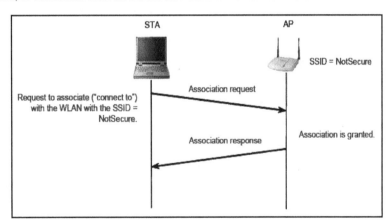

Figure 5-1. Typical Two-Frame IEEE 802.11 Communication

5.1.1   IEEE 802.11 Frame Types

The IEEE 802.11 frame exchange protocol involves three types of frames, as follows:

■ **Data Frame.** Data frames encapsulate packets from upper layer protocols, such as IP, which in turn might contain application data (e.g., e-mail, Web pages). Data frames allow for the delivery of the upper layer protocol packets to a STA or AP. RSNA security mechanisms protect these frames.

■ **Management Frame.** Management frames carry the information necessary for managing the MAC. They provide the ability to perform management functions such as authenticating or associating (the wireless equivalent to connecting or registering). These frames can easily be forged, since IEEE 802.11i does not protect management frames. IEEE 802.11w is working on a standard to protect some management frames.

■ **Control Frame.** Control frames are used for requesting and controlling access to the wireless media. An example of a control frame is the acknowledgement frame, which is used after data frames to ensure reliability. Its primary purpose is to alert the sender that the last frame was received correctly and there is no need to retransmit. This simple positive acknowledgement following each frame is expected, or the frame is considered lost. These frames can easily be forged, since IEEE 802.11i does not protect control frames.

Table 5-1 lists the 11 subtypes of management frames, most of which are applicable only in IEEE 802.11 infrastructure mode (i.e., when STAs connect to an AP rather than directly to other STAs). A brief description of each frame is provided in the table. All of these frame subtypes are part of pre-RSN IEEE 802.11; however, some have been modified by the IEEE 802.11i amendment to allow for the establishment of RSNs. The frames that have been modified are identified by a check ($\checkmark$).

Table 5-1. IEEE 802.11 Management Frame Subtypes

Frame Subtype	Description	Modified in IEEE 802.11i
Association Request	Used by a STA to request an association. The SSID is provided in this frame.	$\checkmark$
Association Response	Used to indicate the status (success or failure) of the Association Request.	
Reassociation Request	Used by a STA that has been associated with one BSS to request an association with another BSS with the same SSID. This frame includes the same information as the Association Request, with the addition of the current AP address.	$\checkmark$
Reassociation Response	Used to indicate the status (success or failure) of the Reassociation Request.	
Probe Request	Used by a STA to locate a WLAN quickly. This frame may be used to locate any WLAN or one with a particular SSID.	
Probe Response	Used by an AP to respond to a Probe Request. This frame contains essentially the same information as a beacon.	$\checkmark$
Beacon	Transmitted periodically by an AP to allow STAs to locate and identify a BSS.	$\checkmark$
Authentication	Used by an AP or STA to verify the identity of another STA.	
Deauthentication	Used by a STA to indicate termination of an authentication relationship.	
Disassociation	Used by a STA to indicate termination of an association.	
Announcement Traffic Indication Message (ATIM)	Used by a STA in an IBSS to notify other STAs that may have been operating in low power modes that it has data buffered and waiting to be delivered to the STA addressed in the ATIM frame.	

Figure 5-2 illustrates the flow of management frames in a frame exchange between three STAs and an AP in a single infrastructure BSS. The AP periodically sends a Beacon frame, alerting all stations that the WLAN is operating in the area. After completing an IEEE 802.11 authentication exchange, the STAs are then able to connect to the AP by associating with it. STA 1 and STA 2 perform the Association Request-Response frame exchange with the AP to accomplish the STA registration for later frame delivery from the DS. STA 3 joins the network after the beacon was transmitted. As a result, it sends a Probe Request frame—an active request for WLANs in the area—to determine the capabilities of the AP, and receives a Probe Response frame containing the requested information. Section 5.2 provides additional descriptions of the Beacon, Association, and Probe frames.

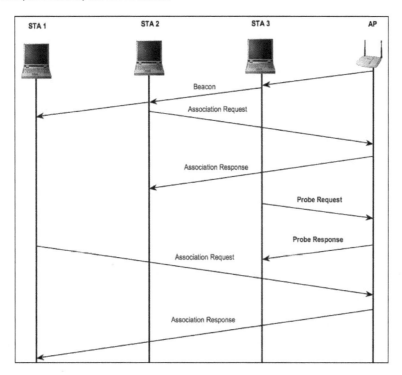

Figure 5-2. Multi-STA WLAN Flow Diagram

5.1.2 IEEE 802.11 Data Frame Structure

Figure 5-3 depicts the IEEE 802.11 data frame structure. As shown, the data frame begins with a MAC header, which contains numerous fields for the transport of data in a WLAN. Most importantly, the header provides the MAC addresses of the source and destination, as well as the transmitter address, which identifies the address of the wireless network interface card that transmitted the frame onto the wireless medium, and the receiver address, which identifies the wireless station or group address that should process the frame. For example, when APs bridge wired LANs, a STA can send a message to a wired LAN end station connected to the AP, in which case the receiver address is the AP's address, and the destination address is the end station's address. Each STA and AP processes frames with a receiver address that matches its MAC address. Each AP also forwards frames to an attached LAN when a frame's destination address is different than the receiver address. In addition to the MAC addresses and other header fields, a data frame also contains a frame body, which is the encapsulated data from the higher layer protocol, and a frame check sequence (FCS), which is provided for error detection purposes.

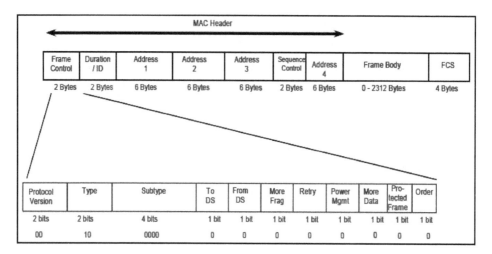

Figure 5-3. IEEE 802.11 Frame Format

The following items briefly describe the frame body, FCS, and MAC header fields.

- **Frame Body.** This field, also called the Data field, holds a payload from a higher layer. The Frame Body field is variable in length, with a maximum size of 2312 octets.[47]

- **FCS.** This field is used for error detection to detect random bit errors in the received frame. It contains the result of applying a 32-bit cyclic redundancy check (CRC-32) on the data. Because of this, the FCS is often called the CRC. The FCS calculation is performed on all data in the MAC header and frame body.

- **Frame Control Field.** As shown in Figure 5-3, this field defines a number of parameters for IEEE 802.11 operation. For example, it contains two bits used to identify the version of the IEEE 802.11 MAC. Another value within the field is the Protected Frame bit; if it is set to 1, the frame body is cryptographically protected using the negotiated ciphersuite (e.g., CCMP, TKIP, WEP).[48] The Frame Control Field also indicates the frame type (e.g., management, control, data) and subtype (e.g., Association Request, Probe Response).[49]

- **Duration/ID.** This field is used by a STA to retrieve frames buffered at an AP. The field identifies the remaining duration in the frame exchange between a STA and AP.

- **Sequence Control.** This field is used to allow a STA to identify received frames that are duplicates, and to assist it in reassembling fragmented frames.

- **Address Fields.** The MAC header for a data frame contains four distinct address fields, although in some cases not all fields contain relevant addresses. The address fields identify the original source address (SA) and final destination address (DA) in a frame exchange, as well as the receiver address (RA). Depending on the function of the frame, the address fields also identify either the transmitter address (TA) or the BSS identifier (BSSID), which is typically the address of the AP. The sequence of the addresses in the MAC header depends on two things: whether the transmitting station is in an IBSS or an infrastructure BSS, and whether the communicating

---

[47] An octet is 8 bits

[48] Prior to the IEEE 802 11i amendment, the Protected Frame field was called the WEP field The name was changed to account for the new data confidentiality and integrity protocols defined in IEEE 802 11i

[49] For additional details on the IEEE 802 11 frame structure, consult the IEEE 802 11 standard or textbooks on the subject

stations are part of the DS. Table 5-2 identifies the functions of each of the address fields for the four possible cases, as defined by the values for the To DS and From DS subfields.

Table 5-2. MAC Header Address Field Functions for Data Frames

Function	"To DS" Subfield	"From DS" Subfield[50]	Address 1	Address 2	Address 3	Address 4
IBSS	0	0	RA = DA	SA	BSSID	N/A
Infrastructure BSS: From the AP	0	1	RA = DA	BSSID	SA	N/A
Infrastructure BSS: To the AP	1	0	RA = BSSID	SA	DA	N/A
Infrastructure BSS: Wireless DS (AP to AP)	1	1	RA	TA	DA	SA

5.2   Phases of IEEE 802.11 RSN Operation

This section provides an overview of the operation of an IEEE 802.11 RSN. By grouping the frame exchanges according to function, RSN operation may be thought of as occurring in five distinct phases, some of which also occur in pre-RSN IEEE 802.11 implementations. Figure 5-4 depicts the phases in an infrastructure mode configuration and maps them to the WLAN network components involved in each phase, as well as end stations outside the WLAN RSN in the distribution system (e.g., other computers in the wired network). The rectangles represent the sequence of frames between the network components.

The following items briefly describe each of the phases.

- **Phase 1: Discovery.** An AP uses Beacons and Probe Responses to advertise its IEEE 802.11i security policy. The STA uses these to identify an AP for a WLAN with which it wishes to communicate. The STA associates with the AP, which it uses to select the cipher suite and authentication mechanism when the Beacons and Probe Responses present a choice.

- **Phase 2: Authentication.** During this phase, the STA and AS prove their identities to each other. The AP blocks non-authentication traffic between the STA and AS until the authentication transaction is successful. The AP does not participate in the authentication transaction other than forwarding traffic between the STA and AS.

- **Phase 3: Key Generation and Distribution.** The AP and the STA perform several operations that cause cryptographic keys to be generated and placed on the AP and the STA. Frames are exchanged between the AP and STA only.

- **Phase 4: Protected Data Transfer.** Frames are exchanged between the STA and the end station through the AP. As denoted by the shading and the lock and key, secure data transfer occurs between the STA and the AP only; security is not provided end-to-end.

- **Phase 5: Connection Termination.** The AP and STA exchange frames. During this phase, the secure connection is torn down and the connection is restored to the original state.

Sections 5.3 through 5.7 provide in-depth discussion of each phase.

---

[50]   Figure 5-3 shows the To DS and From DS fields

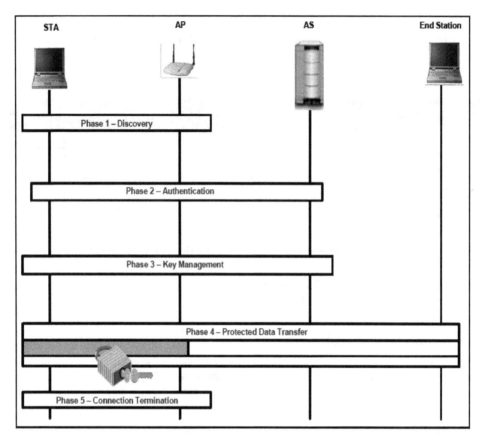

Figure 5-4. Five Phases of Operation

5.3 Discovery Phase

The discovery phase is the first phase in the process to establish RSNAs. During this phase, STAs discover the existence of a network with which to communicate. STAs locate and identify APs through the APs' periodic transmission of Beacon frames.[51] A Beacon frame contains a timestamp, beacon interval, and capability information, which includes supported data rates and the SSID. Figure 5-5 depicts an ESS with three APs; each has a different SSID. Because the STA shown with the ellipse is within the range of all three APs, it can identify and connect (associate) with any of them.

During the discovery phase, STAs and APs negotiate several things, including the SSID, supported data rates, and other technical operating parameters related to reliable communication, as well as a security policy. In general, 802.11i does not support extensive negotiation The AP describes the options that it supports, and only clients that are configured for compatible options will attempt to connect. Many APs and STAs can only store a single configuration at a time. Section 5.3.1 provides a detailed explanation of the security policy negotiation process. Section 5.3.2 shows how frames used for negotiation flow between STAs and APs during the discovery phase.

---

[51] Beacon frames may be configured to transmit periodically from approximately every millisecond to every 66 seconds

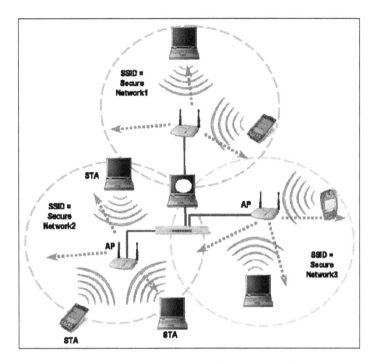

Figure 5-5. Beacons Used During the Discovery Phases in an ESS

5.3.1 Establishing a Security Policy

During the discovery phase, STAs and APs negotiate the following key security capabilities:

■ Confidentiality and integrity protocols for protecting unicast traffic

■ Authentication method for mutual authentication of the AP and AS

■ Cryptographic key management approach

■ Pre-authentication capabilities (described in more detail in Section 5.4.4).

Confidentiality and integrity protocols for protecting multicast/broadcast traffic are dictated by the AP, since all STAs in a multicast group must use the same cipher suite.

The specification of the confidentiality and integrity protocol, along with the chosen key length (if variable), is known as the *cipher suite*. The same cipher suite options are available for protecting unicast traffic and multicast and broadcast traffic.[52] The possible cipher suites allowed by the IEEE 802.11i amendment are as follows:

■ WEP, with either a 40-bit or 104-bit key

■ TKIP

■ CCMP, which is the default choice according to the 802.11i standard. In practice, many existing devices default to TKIP.

---

[52] The WEP cipher suites are only valid as a group cipher suite in a Transition Security Network to allow pre-RSNA devices to join a BSS. They are not valid in an RSN.

- Vendor-specific methods (to allow for flexibility and expansion).

As listed below, there are three options for what the IEEE 802.11 standard refers to as Authentication and Key Management (AKM). An *AKM suite* defines the means by which the AP and STAs are mutually authenticated during initial operation and the means for deriving the root key shown in the Pairwise Key Hierarchy. RSNAs may be established for WLANs in either ad hoc mode (IBSS) or infrastructure mode (BSS) using any of the AKM suites. The possible AKM suites are as follows:

- Mutual authentication and key management over IEEE 802.1X or using pairwise master key security association (PMKSA) caching, which is discussed in more detail in Section 5.4.4. Authentication is accomplished with an EAP method. If a specific AKM suite is not supplied during security policy negotiation, this suite will be used as the default AKM suite.

- Pre-shared key. No explicit authentication transaction takes place. If the PSK is unique for each STA, the STA and AP effectively authenticate each other by holding an identical pre-shared key, without which the data confidentiality and integrity services could not function properly. In practice, many PSK APs use a single PSK for every STA. This means that, rather than authenticating the client, the AP is verifying that the client is a member of an authorized group (the group that shares the key). The actual identity of the client has not been established, so this is not client authentication in the normal meaning of the term. However, the STA does authenticate the AP.

- Proprietary suites developed by vendors; this allows for flexibility and expansion.

A security association between a STA and an AP is a relationship established between these two entities that enable them to protect data the exchange. Both entities store the security association information, which includes the set of security policies and cryptographic keys used to protect the data (e.g., SSID, the specific PMK, MAC addresses). An AP that is prepared to establish a RSNA will broadcast (advertise) its capabilities, including its supported encryption and authentication capabilities. The capabilities are included in a field called the *RSN Information Element (RSNIE)*, which is part of Beacon and Probe Response frames.[53] Figure 5-6 depicts the fields of the RSNIE. As shown, the RSNIE also conveys the group key cipher suite, pairwise cipher suite, and AKM suite. For example, an RSNIE could specify a group key cipher suite of CCMP, a pairwise cipher suite of CCMP, and an AKM suite of IEEE 802.1X. The RSN Capabilities field includes an indication of whether Pre-Authentication is possible and whether WEP with a default key is possible.

---

[53] All the management frames listed in Table 5-1 with the checkmarks contain the RSNIE

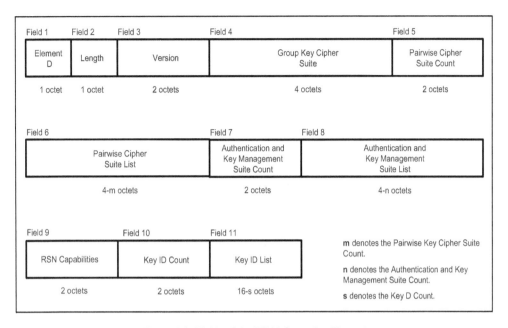

Figure 5-6. Fields of the RSN Information Element

5.3.2 Discovery Phase Frame Flows

Figure 5-7 depicts the flow of the three Request-Response pairs that comprise the discovery phase. In this scenario, the STA sends a Probe Request frame to locate an AP in the area. The AP responds with its capabilities in the RSNIE field of the Probe Response frame; this includes all of its enabled encryption and authentication capabilities. When the STA receives the Probe Response frame, it performs open system authentication—null authentication—with the AP. The purpose of this frame sequence, which provides no security, is simply to maintain backward compatibility with the IEEE 802.11 state machine,[54] as implemented in existing IEEE 802.11 hardware.

Following the authentication frame exchange, the STA then sends an Association Request frame to the AP. In this frame, the STA specifies one set of matching capabilities (one authentication and key management suite, one pairwise cipher suite, and one group key cipher suite) from among those advertised by the AP. If there is no match in capabilities between the AP and the STA, the AP refuses the Associate Request. The STA blocks it too, in case it has associated with a rogue AP or someone is inserting frames illicitly on its channel. As shown in the figure, the IEEE 802.1X controlled ports are blocked, and no user traffic goes beyond the AP. This process of mutually advertising and agreeing on the security capabilities is referred to as *security policy negotiation*.

---

[54] The term *state machine* refers to a structured software algorithm that performs a particular function in electronic equipment In this case, the algorithm is that which performs IEEE 802.11 communications

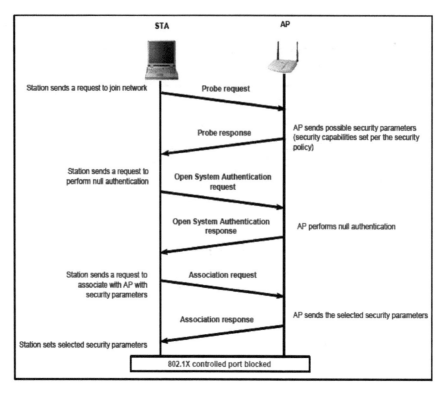

Figure 5-7. Discovery Phase Frame Flows

As an alternative to the frame flow depicted in Figure 5-7, the Probe Request-Response pair may be absent. If the STA had monitored one of the periodic Beacon frames from the AP, it would not have needed to request the parameters from the AP through a Probe Request. Therefore, a STA can discover an AP's security policy through either or both of two methods: passively monitoring for AP Beacon frames, and actively probing for all APs within range.

Figure 5-8 depicts an example of security policy negotiation. As shown, the AP advertises its capabilities to the STA in a periodic Beacon frame, as set by the WLAN security policy. In this example, the AP informs the STA that it is capable of performing IEEE 802.1X authentication, CCMP for unicast traffic protection, and CCMP for broadcast traffic protection.[55] The STA also indicates that it is capable of performing IEEE 802.1X authentication and CCMP for both types of traffic. At this point, the AP accepts the IEEE 802.1X and CCMP request, then self-configures these capabilities. It confirms its declaration with an Association Response frame, indicating the completion of security policy negotiation and the end of the discovery phase.

---

[55] The IEEE 802.11i amendment states that if CCMP is used for broadcast traffic protection, then TKIP cannot be used for unicast traffic

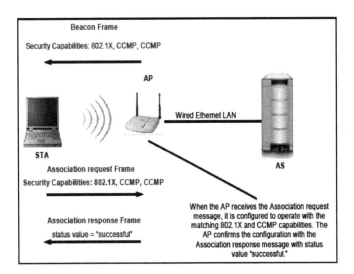

Figure 5-8. Conceptual Example of Security Policy Negotiation

During the discovery phase, a STA may decline to communicate with an AP or another STA that fails to disclose any of the following:

■ Security policy in the Beacon or Probe Response frames

■ Authorized SSID

■ Authorized encryption and authentication cipher suites.

The IEEE 802.11 standard does not specify the manner in which these conditions are handled. This remains undefined and is left as a design choice to the RSN technology manufacturer. Manufacturers typically design their products so that these conditions are configurable via policy.

5.3.3 Distinguishing RSN and Pre-RSN WLANs

The outcome of the discovery phase is very important to the security posture of a WLAN. In an RSN, APs do not allow associations from pre-RSN STAs—those STAs that do not support data confidentiality and integrity mechanisms beyond WEP and that cannot create PMK security associations. For example, an ESS might contain several IEEE 802.11 STAs and three APs. Suppose that all STAs within this ESS use pre-shared keying (as opposed to the IEEE 802.1X technique) and the CCMP security method for both unicast and broadcast traffic. These parameters are negotiated through the discovery phase's security parameter negotiation. Because the three APs have allowed only RSNAs with the seven STAs, they provide an RSN.

In contrast, suppose that the STAs in the ESS do not all operate with CCMP; two are using pre-RSN capabilities. These stations, forming a Transition Security Network, are using WEP and shared key authentication. As a result, this WLAN is not an RSN, even though five of its STAs are operating with CCMP. The two STAs using pre-RSN capabilities create significant security holes that can negatively impact the security of the other components of the WLAN. Not only are the communications between the STA and AP not protected strongly, but also the AP must be configured to permit the use of pre-RSN capabilities. This could allow an attacker within range of the AP to establish unauthorized connections to it, potentially gaining access to other resources.

5.4   Authentication Phase

Upon successful completion of the discovery phase, the STA and AP enter the second phase in the establishment of an RSNA: the authentication phase. This phase provides the means for a STA to prove its identity to the WLAN. This security service is critical for preventing unauthorized access to network resources. In an infrastructure WLAN, authentication provides protection against unauthorized users in the DS, since the AP is the entry point into the ESS. Improper authentication can undermine all security measures in an enterprise. Mutual authentication also allows the WLAN to prove its identity to the STA, which allows the STA to validate positively that it is communicating with a legitimate WLAN, as opposed to an unauthorized or "rogue" WLAN.

Figure 5-9 depicts the concept of authentication that occurs during this phase. As shown, the authentication occurs between the STA and the AS, which is located in the DS. This authentication procedure is designed to disallow all stations from using the network except for those that are explicitly authorized to do so. It also provides a level of confidence to the STA's user that the STA is communicating with the legitimate network.

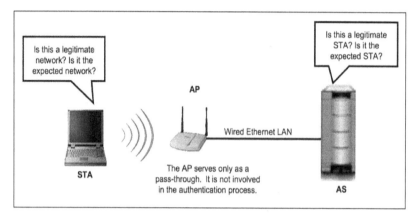

Figure 5-9. Concept of Authentication

5.4.1   The IEEE 802.1X Framework: Port-Based Access Control

As described in Section 3, the IEEE 802.11 standard uses the IEEE 802.1X standard to provide mutual authentication between STAs and ASs. IEEE 802.1X is a general-purpose, extensible framework for authenticating users. The actual authentication mechanism incorporated into the framework is implemented by the STA and the AS using EAP. EAP provides a framework that allows the use of multiple methods for achieving authentication, including static passwords, dynamic passwords (e.g., one-time passwords, token generators), and public key cryptography certificates (on the AS only or on both the AS and STAs). Dozens of standard and proprietary EAP methods exist; Section 6 provides more information on the most commonly used ones.

IEEE 802.1X authentication has three main components: a client (also known as a supplicant), an authenticator, and an AS. The authenticator simply passes authentication traffic between the client and AS. IEEE 802.1X controls the flow of data between the DS and STAs by use of a controlled/uncontrolled port model. EAP authentication occurs through the IEEE 802.1X *uncontrolled port* on the authenticator; non-EAP data frames are passed or blocked via the IEEE 802.1X *controlled port*, depending upon the success or failure of IEEE 802.1X authentication (which includes EAP). This model is known as port-based access control. Using this concept, IEEE 802.1X achieves the objective of blocking access for unauthorized parties in an IEEE 802.11 WLAN.

The authentication message flows between the client and the authenticator typically use the EAP over LAN (EAPOL) protocol. RADIUS is the protocol most commonly used to transport EAP messages between the authenticator and the AS. The steps in a typical successful IEEE 802.1X authentication exchange when RADIUS is used to support authentication-related traffic on the DS are as follows:

1. The supplicant (client) may start the exchange with an optional EAPOL-Start message.

2. The EAP exchange begins with the authenticator issuing an EAP-Request/Identity frame to the supplicant.

3. The supplicant replies with an EAP-Response/Identity frame, which the AP receives over the uncontrolled port. The packet is then encapsulated in RADIUS over EAP and passed on to the RADIUS server as a RADIUS-Access-Request packet.

4. The AAA server replies with a RADIUS-Access-Challenge packet, which is passed on to the supplicant as an EAP-Request. This request is of the appropriate authentication type and contains relevant challenge information.

5. The supplicant formulates an EAP-Response message and sends it to the authenticator. The response is translated by the authenticator into a Radius-Access-Request, with the response to the challenge as a data field. Steps 4 and 5 may be repeated multiple times, depending on the EAP method in use. For TLS tunneling methods, it is common for authentication to require 10-20 round trips.

6. The AAA server grants access with a Radius-Access-Accept packet. The authenticator issues an EAP-Success frame. (Some protocols require confirmation of the EAP success inside the TLS tunnel for authenticity validation.) The controlled port is authorized, and the user may begin to access the network.

7. During the termination phase, when the supplicant is finished accessing the network, it may send an optional EAPOL-Logoff message to restore the controlled port to an unauthorized state.

Figure 5-10 depicts the authentication frame flow in an IEEE 802.11 RSNA. As shown, authentication occurs between the STA and AS, with the AP assisting in the networking dialog. The IEEE 802.1X controlled port is blocked before the EAP authentication procedures take place. The EAP authentication process, which occurs over the IEEE 802.1X uncontrolled port, starts when the AP sends the EAP-Request frame to the STA, or the STA sends the EAPOL-Start frame. EAP frames pass between the STA and the AS via the uncontrolled ports.

At the conclusion of the authentication dialog, the AP controlled port is still blocked to general user traffic. Although the authentication is successful, the ports remain blocked until the temporal keys are installed in the STA and AP, which occurs during the 4-Way Handshake. This blocking keeps unauthorized traffic from entering the DS and prevents any traffic from the DS from being transmitted wirelessly. The STA may also initiate an IEEE 802.1X authentication frame exchange. In this case, the exchange is the same, with the exception that the STA initiates it by issuing an EAPOL-Start message to the AP.

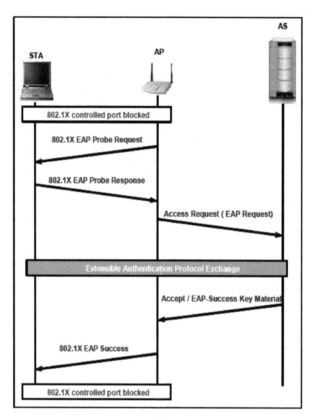

Figure 5-10. Authentication Phase of Operation

After the seven-step authentication process has been completed, the AAA key is installed in the STA and the AS. As discussed in Section 4.2.1, the AAA key serves as a root key to enable the generation of other keys used to secure communications between the STA and the AP. The AAA key for this particular STA is the foundation of security, and its compromise would be devastating to the overall security of the system. The IEEE 802.11 standard does not describe specifically how the MSK is delivered to the AS and STA; it relies on EAP to handle this. RFC 3580, "IEEE 802.1X Remote Authentication Dial In User Service (RADIUS) Usage Guidelines," specifies the method for MSK delivery. Although the IEEE standard does not prescribe a method for secure MSK delivery and installation, it does indicate the importance of the connection between the AS and AP.

5.4.2 Authentication with the PSK

Typically, the authentication phase provides mutual authentication of a STA and an AS in an RSNA and delivers the Master Session Key to the AP and, sometimes, to the STA. However, in an RSNA that has negotiated the PSK AKM during the discovery phase, the authentication phase is not required, because the shared key has already been distributed and installed in an out-of-band manner that has implicitly provided authentication. Therefore, when the AKM is PSK, the authentication phase is skipped entirely, as shown in Figure 5-11. However, the IEEE 802.1X controlled ports are still blocked, preventing users' traffic from being passed to the DS.

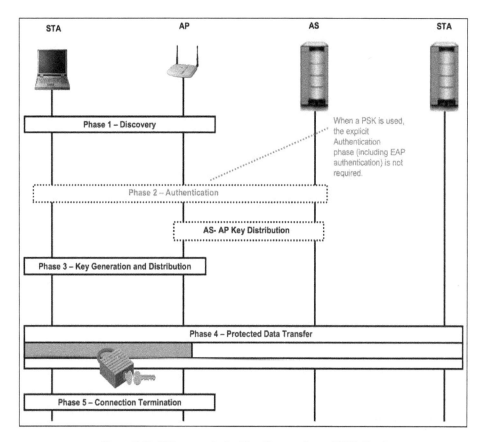

Figure 5-11. Differences in the Five Phases when a PSK Is Used

5.4.3 AS to AP Connections

As shown in Figure 5-4 and Figure 5-11, following the authentication phase of operation, the AS delivers the AAA key to the AP. The data flows from the two network elements are depicted in Figure 5-11 by the dashed rectangle labeled AS-AP Key Distribution. As described in Section 4.2.1, the AAA key is the basis of the Pairwise Transient Key (PTK) and other keys (i.e., TK, EAPOL-KEK, and EAPOL-KCK). The interface between the AS and the AP—to allow the distribution of the AAA key and support mutual authentication—is not fully defined in the IEEE 802.11i specification. However, RADIUS and Diameter are the protocols most likely to be used to support authentication traffic between an AS and AP.

Although the details of the communications interface between the AS and the AP are outside the scope of the IEEE 802.11i amendment, the amendment does contain several requirements for the interface to ensure that the security of an RSN is not compromised. Specifically, the communication link between the AS and AP must provide the following:

■ Robust, mutual authentication between the AS and AP

■ An end-to-end channel between the AS and the authenticator for the mutual authentication

■ The ability to transfer the cryptographic key generated by the AS to the AP securely. As shown in Figure 5-12, the AS to AP communication must provide confidentiality and integrity, and the AS must prevent key compromise during storage.

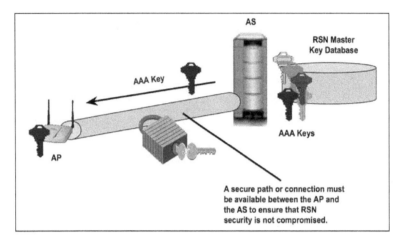

Figure 5-12. AP to AS Communication

The AS is a critical component of overall RSN security. The IEEE 802.11 standard assumes the following with respect to the AS:

■ It does not expose or compromise the PMK (a subset of the AAA key) to other entities besides the AP.

■ It does not masquerade as a STA to the AP.

■ It does not masquerade as an AP to the STA.

Figure 5-13 depicts a typical enterprise environment with numerous STAs and APs, plus a single AS to provide authentication services during the third phase of RSN establishment. A AAA server running RADIUS is commonly used as the AS, but other types of AAA servers such as those supporting Diameter may also perform the service. In some small or single AP implementations, the AS may be physically integrated into the AP. In that case, there is no external communication for EAP authentication or for delivery of the AAA key.

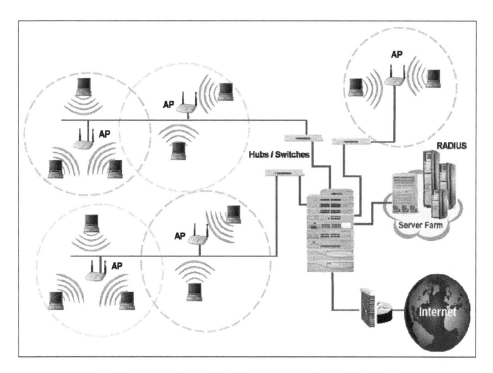

Figure 5-13. Typical Enterprise with Multiple APs, STAs, and an AS

5.4.4 Pre-Authentication and PMKSA Caching

Pre-Authentication and PMKSA caching (also referred to as PMK caching or Proactive Key Caching) are mechanisms that improve performance, particularly in roaming scenarios. In Pre-Authentication, a STA can initiate an EAP over IEEE 802.1X authentication transaction with an AP outside of radio range using an association with another AP and the DS for communication. This procedure creates a PMKSA between the STA and remote AP. The PMKSA is cached (i.e., stored in a state table in memory) on both the STA and remote AP. When the STA enters within range of the previously remote AP, it can initiate a 4-Way Handshake without a successful IEEE 802.1X and EAP authentication transaction, which occurred earlier over the DS. The Pre-Authentication capability enables roaming STAs to start data communications more quickly than if full authentication were required for every association. Although pre-authentication is defined in 802.11i, it is not widely implemented.

PMKSA caching can also be enabled to improve performance even in the absence of Pre-Authentication. If a STA in a fixed location often loses its connection to an AP due to radio interference or other reasons, PMKSAs can enable quick reassociation without requiring the full authentication process.

If PMKSA caching is enabled, the STA supplies a list of PMKSAs to the authenticator during an association or reassociation frame exchange. If the authenticator finds a match, then IEEE 802.1X and EAP authentication is not necessary, and the STA and AP can start the 4-Way Handshake using the cached PMKSA. If the AP does not have a corresponding PMKSA for the supplicant, then it will require the full IEEE 802.1X and EAP authentication process. If the 4-Way Handshake fails, both sides can remove the associated cached PMKSA.

5.5 Key Generation and Distribution

Following the successful completion of the authentication phase, the STA and AP perform a series of functions that position cryptographic keys in both entities. This phase is called the key generation and distribution (KGD) phase. It provides the final step in authentication and allows the STA and AP to derive keys that make secure data transfer possible. The KGD phase has several purposes, including the following:

- Confirming the existence of the Pairwise Master Key (PMK)

- Ensuring the security association keys are new

- Deriving and synchronizing the installation of traffic encryption keys (temporal keys) in the AP and STA

- Distributing a group key for multicast and broadcast traffic protection

- Confirming the cipher suite selection.

The KGD phase includes two types of handshakes: a 4-Way Handshake and a Group Handshake. The Group Handshake is necessary only when STAs participate in multicast or broadcast traffic. Both types of handshakes employ the following fundamental security features:

- Message integrity checking, to protect against tampering and to validate the source of traffic

- Message encryption, to protect against unauthorized disclosure of data.

The confidentiality and integrity algorithms used for both handshakes are configurable to either of the following:

- **RC4 Encryption with HMAC-MD5.** RC4 is the well-known stream cipher that forms the basis of WEP. RC4 uses the 128-bit EAPOL-KEK derived from the PTK using the PRF.

- **AES Key Wrap[56] with HMAC-SHA-1-128.** The AES Key Wrap was designed specifically to encrypt keying material (cryptographic keys). The key wrap parses data into n blocks of 64-bits and "wraps" (encrypts) the key contents. The key wrap uses the AES codebook mode along with the EAPOL-KEK derived from the PTK.

Both RC4 and the AES Key Wrap use the HMAC along with the EAPOL-KCK derived from the PTK using the PRF to provide integrity during the 4-Way Handshake. As discussed in Section 2, Federal agencies are required to use encryption algorithms that are FIPS-approved. RC4 encryption and MD5 are not FIPS-approved, but AES and SHA-1 are, so NIST requires that Federal agencies use AES Key Wrap with HMAC-SHA-1-128 instead of RC4 encryption with HMAC-MD5.

5.5.1 4-Way Handshake

The KGD phase begins with the 4-Way Handshake, which is depicted in Figure 5-14. During the handshake, four frames are exchanged between the STA and the AP. To generate data for the frames and verify data received in frames, both the STA and the AP perform several computations. At the successful conclusion of the 4-Way Handshake, the AP and STA have been mutually authenticated. At that point, the IEEE 802.1X controlled ports are opened to allow the flow of frames for data traffic.

---

[56] The AES Key Wrap is specified in RFC 3394, *Advanced Encryption Standard (AES) Key Wrap Algorithm*, available at http://www.ietf.org/rfc/rfc3394.txt

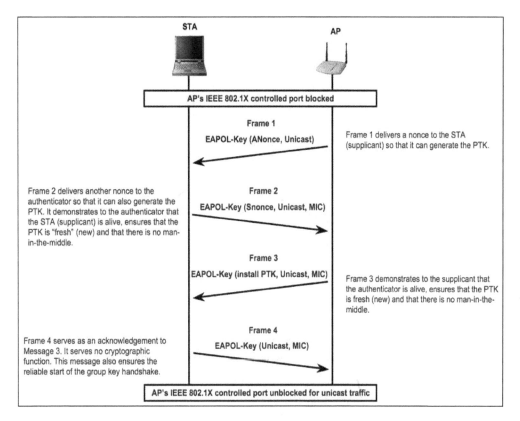

Figure 5-14. 4-Way Handshake

Frames 2, 3 and 4 in the exchange are protected from modification using a message integrity code (MIC) applied to the frames. This message integrity feature, which is mandatory for all frames except the first frame, is performed by computing a message integrity check over the entire frame and sending the MIC along with the frame. Although Frame 1 is not integrity-protected, any modification to it can be detected by the subsequent checking mechanisms. Message encryption is performed to protect critical data from unauthorized disclosure. It may also be used in frame 2 to encrypt the RSNIE; however, this is optional.

5.5.2 Group Key Handshake

The Group Key Handshake is used by the AP to send a new GTK to a STA. It may occur immediately after the 4-Way Handshake or upon STA initiation. It is necessary to support multicast or broadcast traffic. Figure 5-15 depicts the simple two-frame Group Key Handshake.

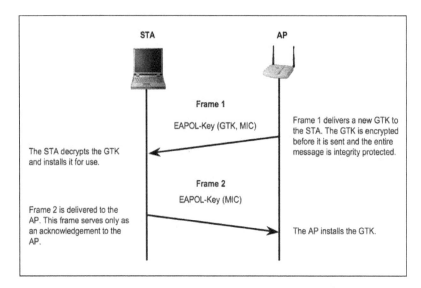

Figure 5-15. Group Key Handshake

After the Group Key Handshake is complete, the AP and STA are ready for operation. The Group Key Handshake also may be used to distribute subsequent GTKs. The AP can use the handshake to update the GTK in STAs under the following conditions:

■ On disassociation or deauthentication of a STA

■ Upon occurrence of an event on the STA that triggers an update, such as a configuration change in the STA's local security policy.

The GMK used to derive the GTK may be updated in the AP at a time interval configured into the system. Periodic updating of the GMK may be included in the security policy for the WLAN. Organizations should update the GMK to prevent exposure of subsequent traffic between STAs and the AP, if the GMK is ever compromised.

5.6   Protected Data Exchange

The fourth phase in the operation of an RSN is the protected data exchange phase. Before this phase, the AP and STA have already done the following:

■ Become associated and negotiated a security policy (discovery phase)

■ Mutually authenticated using EAP and derived a Master Session Key using the uncontrolled IEEE 802.1X port, or implicitly authenticated through a previously installed preshared key (authentication phase)

■ Generated, distributed and confirmed the session keys through the 4-Way Handshake (KGD phase)

■ Derived a pairwise transient key and unblocked the IEEE 802.1X ports (KGD phase).

These actions have prepared the AP and STA to communicate securely. During the protected data exchange phase, the AP and STA may now share data securely. The traffic between the AP and STA is protected using the data confidentiality and integrity algorithms chosen during the discovery phase. IEEE 802.11i supports three methods of data transfer: unicast, multicast, and broadcast.

For RSNs, unicast (also called "directed") is the type of data transfer used most often during the protected data exchange phase. Unicast data transfer can occur when a unique association exists between the AP and the STA and a pairwise transient key is used for the protection of the traffic. Protections afforded unicast frames include encryption, integrity protection, and replay protection. Additionally, because data forgery is a major security concern in WLANs, unicast frames are equipped with a data origin authentication mechanism that prevents masquerading attacks. The mechanism allows a STA to confirm whether or not a received data frame originated from the claimed STA.

The broadcast and multicast data transfer mechanisms (also called "group") allow for common data to be transferred to multiple devices efficiently. Communication between the AP and the STAs is protected using CCMP. Unique Group Key Handshakes with each STA insert the GTK used with CCMP to protect the data exchanges. Because all STAs share the same GTK, a single breach of the GTK affects all STAs.

5.7 Connection Termination

The fifth and final phase in the operation of an RSNA is the connection termination phase. During this phase, the association between the STA and the AP is deleted, and the wireless connection is terminated. This phase provides the elegant teardown of a connection and a restoration to an initialized state.

During the connection termination phase, the following events occur:

- The AP deauthenticates the STA.

- The security associations, used internally by the AP to keep track of associations between STAs and APs, are deleted.

- The temporal keys used for encrypting and protecting the integrity of data traffic are deleted.

- The IEEE 802.1X controlled port returns to a blocked state so that user traffic cannot pass.

The connection termination phase may be entered in several ways, including the following:

- Radio communication between the STA and AP is lost (e.g., STA moves out of range).

- The 4-Way Handshake or Group Key Handshake times out during execution.

- The RSNIE check during the 4-Way Handshake fails.

- The user powers down the STA or disables the NIC.

- The security policy indicates a termination of the connection (implementation-specific).

This phase restores the AP and STA to an initialized state. If further communication is subsequently required, then these devices begin anew at the discovery phase with the re-discovery of the available resources and capabilities.

5.8 Summary

IEEE 802.11 defines how frames are exchanged between STAs and APs. There are three types of IEEE 802.11 frames, as follows:

- **Data frames**, which encapsulate packets from upper layer protocols, such as IP, which in turn might contain application data (e.g., e-mail, Web pages).

- **Management frames**, which include informational probes and beacons, and messages related to the management of association and authentication events.

- **Control frames**, which are used for requesting and controlling access to the wireless media, such as sending an acknowledgement after receiving a data frame.

By grouping the IEEE 802.11 frame exchanges by function, IEEE 802.11 operation may be thought of as occurring in the following five distinct phases:

- **Phase 1: Discovery.** The STA identifies an AP for a WLAN with which it wishes to communicate. The STA locates an AP either by receiving one of the AP's periodic transmissions of Beacon frames, or by sending a Probe Request to solicit a Probe Response from an AP. After the STA has identified an AP, the STA and the AP exchange frames to negotiate various parameters for their communications. By the end of the phase, the STA and AP have established a security policy that specifies several key security capabilities, such as data confidentiality and integrity protocols for protecting traffic, an authentication method, and a key distribution approach.

- **Phase 2: Authentication.** During this phase, the STA and AS prove their identities to each other. The authentication frames pass through the AP, which also blocks non-authentication traffic from the STA using IEEE 802.1X port-based access control. The actual authentication mechanism is implemented by the STA and AS using EAP, which provides a framework that allows the use of multiple methods for achieving authentication, including static passwords, dynamic passwords, and public key cryptography certificates. After authentication has been completed, the AAA key is installed in the STA and AS; it serves as a root key to enable the generation of other keys used to secure communications between the STA and AP.

- **Phase 3: Key Generation and Distribution (KGD).** During the KGD phase, the AP and the STA perform several operations that cause cryptographic keys to be generated and placed on the AP and the STA. The KGD phase employs two types of handshakes: a 4-Way Handshake and a Group Key Handshake. Both employ message encryption and integrity checking, using one of two confidentiality and integrity algorithms. For both types of handshakes, NIST requires the use of AES Key Wrap with HMAC-SHA-1-128 instead of RC4 encryption with HMAC-MD5 because AES and SHA-1 are FIPS-approved algorithms, and RC4 and MD5 are not.

- **Phase 4: Protected Data Transfer.** The STA and AP share data securely, using the security policy and cryptographic keys established during the first three phases. Because secure data transfer occurs between the STA and the AP only, organizations need to consider carefully the security of the data during the rest of its transit (e.g., on the DS).

- **Phase 5: Connection Termination.** During this phase, the STA and AP tear down their secure connection and delete their association, thereby terminating their wireless connection.

The RSN framework introduces the authentication phase, the key generation and distribution phase, and the connection termination phase into IEEE 802.11 operation. Before the IEEE 802.11i amendment, IEEE 802.11 operation involved rudimentary authentication, but only as part of the discovery phase. The RSN framework also introduces new elements and techniques into the other phases, but the basic nature of the dialog remains the same.

Organizations that want to establish IEEE 802.11 RSNs should configure their APs so that they permit the establishment of RSNAs only. During the discovery phase, if an AP permits a WEP-based association with *any* STA, then not only is that association not an RSNA, but the WLAN is no longer an RSN. *All* associations must be RSNAs for the WLAN to be considered an RSN. Allowing any WEP-based associations creates significant security holes that can negatively impact the security of the other components of the WLAN. The communications between some STAs and APs will not be protected strongly, and having APs configured to permit the use of pre-RSN capabilities could allow attackers within range of the AP to establish unauthorized connections to it, potentially gaining access to other resources.

This page has been left blank intentionally.

6.   Extensible Authentication Protocol

As discussed in Section 4, the Extensible Authentication Protocol (EAP) is used during the authentication phase of an IEEE 802.11 RSN. It provides the authentication framework for IEEE 802.11 RSNs that use 802.1X port-based access control. EAP was first officially defined in RFC 2284,[57] which was released in March 1998. It was revised in June 2004 with the release of RFC 3748.[58] The original EAP RFC focuses primarily on the EAP packet format and message types. The subsequent RFC includes significant new material on the EAP framework, security considerations, and interaction with other protocols.

The protocol was developed to provide authentication services for Point-to-Point Protocol (PPP), the primary link-layer protocol for dial-up connections to IP networks. Before EAP, PPP employed the authentication services of Password Authentication Protocol (PAP) and Challenge-Handshake Authentication Protocol (CHAP). Increasingly, there was a demand to support additional deployed authentication methods, such as One Time Passwords or tokens that issue passcodes. Rather than add new authentication methods to PPP, a protocol was created that could be adapted to new authentication methods as they became available. EAP is the outcome of that effort. As EAP deployment spread to other environments, security flaws were discovered. Attempts were made to define generic EAP security requirements, as well as the security needs applicable to specific environments.

EAP supports a wide variety of authentication methods, also called *EAP methods*. These methods include authentication based on passwords, certificates, smart cards, and tokens. EAP methods can also include combinations of authentication techniques, such as a certificate followed by a password, or the option of using either a smart card or a token. This flexibility means that EAP can integrate with nearly any environment to which a WLAN might connect. EAP's pass-through feature enables an AP to forward authentication messages to and from a back-end authentication infrastructure consisting of one or a small number of ASs, which greatly enhances the scalability and performance of the RSN solution. EAP is also used to enable both peers (supplicant and AS) to agree on the keying material and to distribute the key material that serves as the basis for nearly all of the RSN security protections. The keying material can be mutually derived or distributed by the AS. Subsequently, the AS distributes the keying material to the AP. The keying material is used as (loose) authorization from the AS to AP to signal the AP that the STA is authorized to gain access to the WLAN. The protocol most commonly used to transport back-end EAP authentication and key distribution traffic is RADIUS. In this configuration, EAP conversations are carried within RADIUS packets.

The EAP method or methods deployed in an IEEE 802.11 RSN are critical in determining the security of the resulting solution. IEEE 802.11 does not specify a particular authentication method for RSNs, which gives organizations considerable discretion in choosing which authentication method to employ. However, IEEE 802.11i describes the basic EAP assumptions and requirements that are necessary to enable the IEEE 802.11i security model to hold up. If an organization chooses a weak authentication method or implements a strong method improperly, the EAP implementation could seriously weaken the RSN protections. Moreover, if the EAP implementation is also used to support integrated or single sign-on in an enterprise, security breaches could compromise other network assets as well.

This section provides guidance to assist organizations in planning their EAP implementations. The section first discusses common EAP methods and explains how organizations can select EAP methods appropriate to their environment. The section next examines additional EAP security considerations. The last part of the section introduces the EAP architectural model and related support requirements.

---

[57]   RFC 2284, *PPP Extensible Authentication Protocol (EAP)*, is available for download from http://www.ietf.org/rfc/rfc2284.txt

[58]   RFC 3748, *Extensible Authentication Protocol (EAP)*, is available at http://www.ietf.org/rfc/rfc3748.txt

6.1 EAP Methods

EAP methods perform the authentication transaction and generate the key material used to protect subsequent communications. Because of the extensible nature of EAP, dozens of EAP methods exist, and others are being developed. The specifications for some of the EAP methods most commonly used in WLAN environments are available publicly as peer-reviewed or privately submitted IETF Internet-Drafts or RFCs.[59] This enables software developers from various organizations to write implementations of the EAP methods for WLAN products. Once an EAP method is expected to be in common use, the Internet Assigned Numbers Authority (IANA) assigns it a method type code, which effectively adds it to a universally accepted directory of EAP methods.[60] To date, IANA has allocated method type codes to approximately 40 EAP methods. The EAP software on each device knows which method to invoke based on the method type code in the incoming EAP packet.

EAP methods support a number of different types of authentication. For example, authentication might involve a user-defined password entered into a dialog box, a one-time password read from a hardware token, or a certificate stored on a smart card or USB device. Also, while authentication between a STA and an AS is mutual, it is not necessarily symmetric. For example, the AS might authenticate to the STA using a certificate, but the STA might authenticate to the AS with a user-supplied biometric. In all these cases, the nature of the authentication depends on the EAP method employed.

To protect against certain types of attacks, EAP only allows one authentication method to be used in each EAP conversation, but complex authentication architectures can still be supported within this framework. *EAP multiplexing* is the ability of an EAP server to handle multiple EAP methods and distinguish between each EAP conversation when more than one is occurring at the same time. EAP multiplexing enables an organization to require different authentication methods for different applications or user populations. *EAP tunneling* allows the nesting of one or more EAP methods within another EAP method, which in effect requires one type of authentication to be dependent on another in the context of a single EAP conversation. For example, through the use of EAP tunneling, a STA may use one or more techniques to authenticate to the AS, while the AS uses another technique to authenticate to the STA. As discussed later in this section, many of the leading EAP methods for WLAN are tunneled methods.

The remainder of this section discusses how EAP methods are used in practice and describes particular EAP methods and their relative advantages and disadvantages. Section 6.1.1 reviews the EAP method requirements for WLANs. Section 6.1.2 discusses the baseline EAP methods included in RFC 3748, and Section 6.1.3 describes the EAP methods most commonly used in WLAN environments. Finally, Section 6.1.4 summarizes and compares the EAP methods discussed in Sections 6.1.2 and 6.1.3.

6.1.1 EAP Method Requirements for WLANs

EAP methods can support authentication in a wide range of environments, including dial-up networking services and cellular telephony, but not all EAP methods are appropriate for IEEE 802.11 RSNs. This section reviews EAP method requirements for WLANs. It is based largely on RFC 4017, *Extensible Authentication Protocol (EAP) Method Requirements for Wireless LANs,*[61] which is expected to guide industry development of new EAP methods for WLAN applications.

---

[59] Of the EAP methods commonly used with IEEE 802 11, only EAP-SIM has achieved RFC status (RFC 4186, http://www.ietf org/rfc/rfc4186 txt) The IETF EMU Working Group (http://www ietf org/html charters/emu-charter html) is developing an EAP-TLS Internet Draft

[60] For the complete list of EAP methods, see the EAP Registry at http://www iana org/assignments/eap-numbers

[61] RFC 4017 is available at http://www ietf org/rfc/rfc4017 txt

Some EAP methods have security features that other methods do not. To help people understand the level of security that an EAP method provides, RFC 3748 includes a list of security claims, which are essentially security protection goals that an EAP method might meet. Since the publication of RFC 3748 in June 2004, EAP methods entering the IETF RFC process must include a statement of which RFC 3748 security claims apply to the method and which do not. In addition, the specification for the EAP method should include a justification for the claims that it makes, perhaps through a formal proof, so that users of the EAP method can assess the level of assurance behind the claim. RFC 4017 identifies the security claims that are mandatory, recommended, and optional for WLANs. Table 6-1 summarizes the result of that effort.

Table 6-1. Security Claims for EAP Methods Used in WLANs (Part 1 of 2)

Security Claim	Requirement Level	Explanation of Claim
Key derivation	Mandatory	*Key derivation* is the ability of the EAP method to derive the exportable key material that will be used for IEEE 802.11 RSN cryptographic protections.[62]
Key strength	Mandatory	*Key strength* is a measure of the strength of the key derivation claim, expressed in a number of bits.[63]
Mutual authentication	Mandatory	*Mutual authentication* occurs when the STA authenticates the AS and the AS authenticates the STA in the same EAP exchange using a particular EAP method. Two independent one-way methods do not necessarily constitute mutual authentication.
Shared state equivalence[64]	Mandatory	*Shared state equivalence* means that the EAP peer and server must share state attributes associated with the EAP method, including the method version number, the credentials provided and accepted, and any other negotiated method-specific state attributes. Both parties must be able to distinguish one instance of the method from another.
Dictionary attack resistance	Mandatory	A password-based EAP method provides *resistance against dictionary attacks* if it does not allow an attacker to capture EAP traffic and then use a dictionary of common passwords to guess the password.
Man-in-the-middle attack resistance[65]	Mandatory	An EAP method provides *man-in-the-middle attack resistance* if an attacker cannot use a WLAN device to proxy communication successfully between a STA and AP in an unauthorized manner. In man-in-the-middle attacks, the adversary's device impersonates the STA when communicating with the AP and impersonates the AP when communicating with the STA.

---

[62] IEEE 802.11i-compliant WLAN equipment will not be able to function with EAP methods that cannot satisfy the key derivation claim because the WLAN software on the WLAN equipment needs the key material to perform subsequent transactions. This distinguishes the key derivation claim from other security claims; methods that cannot make the other security claims will provide inadequate protection, but will not cause system failure.

[63] Per RFC 4017, an EAP method suitable for use in an IEEE 802.11 RSN must generate key material with at least 128 bits of effective key strength (as defined in Section 7.2.1 of RFC 3748) and must export a Master Session Key (MSK) and an Extended Master Session Key (EMSK) of at least 512 bits each (as noted in RFC 3748, Section 7.10).

[64] This claim is not defined in RFC 3748, Section 7.2.1, but appears as a mandatory requirement in RFC 4017.

[65] Man-in-the-middle attack resistance corresponds to the cryptographic binding, integrity protection, replay protection, and session independence security claims defined in RFC 3748, Section 7.2.1. These claims are combined into a single requirement in RFC 4017. Protection against man-in-the-middle attacks can be provided through several means, including cryptographic binding, session independence, replay protection, or integrity protection. In cryptographic binding, a unique identifier from each entity is included in the key generation process in such a way as to guarantee that the parties to a communication did not change during the communication session. Session independence, often referred to as forward and reverse secrecy, is realized when an attacker cannot compromise the key material from subsequent or prior sessions from a compromise of any given session. Replay protection is achieved when a unique element such as a counter value is used in key generation. The result is that unique keys are used for each transaction, which prevents an attacker from capturing one session and replaying it at a later time. Integrity protection refers to the use of cryptography to provide data origin authentication and protection against unauthorized modification of EAP packets.

Table 6-1. Security Claims for EAP Methods Used in WLANs (Part 2 of 2)

Security Claim	Requirement Level	Explanation of Claim
Protected ciphersuite negotiation	Mandatory	*Protected ciphersuite negotiation* refers to the negotiation of a cryptographic algorithm and key to protect the confidentiality and integrity of the EAP conversation. This claim does not refer to the ciphersuite used to protect subsequent data traffic.
Packet fragmentation and reassembly	Recommended	*Packet fragmentation and reassembly* enables an EAP method to handle messages larger than EAP's Maximum Transmission Unit (MTU) limit of 1020 octets.[66]
Confidentiality	Recommended	*Confidentiality* refers to encryption of EAP messages, including EAP Requests and Responses, success and failure result indications, and user identities.
Channel binding	Optional	*Channel binding* can be used to ensure that the authenticator, when in pass-through mode, is validated and not impersonated. One way of achieving this is using media access control (MAC) addresses or other endpoint identifiers as inputs to the key generation process, which helps ensure that entities other than the endpoints in the EAP conversation do not participate in that conversation.
Fast reconnect	Optional	*Fast reconnect* refers to the ability of an EAP method to refresh a previously established security association with fewer messages than required to create the initial association.[67]

In the context of an IEEE 802.11 RSN, man-in-the-middle attack resistance can be among the most difficult of the claims to establish. In a typical configuration, the AP resides between the STA and AS, and the AS authenticates the AP, using the RADIUS shared secret, during the EAP exchange. An authorized and weakly authenticated man-in-the-middle exists under normal operating conditions. In this environment, an attacker can easily defeat weak authentication methods by setting up a rogue AP. Therefore, it is critical that appropriate EAP methods be selected to eliminate this risk. As Section 6.1.2 explains, the EAP methods defined in RFC 3748 are vulnerable to man-in-the-middle attacks. Section 6.1.3 discusses EAP methods that can eliminate the risk of such attacks if implemented properly.

6.1.2   RFC 3748-Defined EAP Methods

RFC 3748 establishes how EAP functions and also defines the following three EAP methods, which are described later in this section:

- MD5-Challenge

- One-Time Password (OTP)

- Generic Token Card (GTC).

Other IETF RFCs and Internet-Drafts define additional EAP methods. RFC 3748 requires that all EAP implementations support the MD5-Challenge method; support for the other two methods is optional. None of the RFC 3748 methods can meet any of the WLAN-required security claims. In some cases, however, the RFC 3748 methods are tunneled within the TLS methods discussed in Section 6.1.3.

---

[66]   Packet fragmentation and reassembly services ensure proper functioning of the authentication transaction. Failure to support this claim might enable an adversary to exploit unintended behavior resulting from large packets, which could include bypassing authentication protections or causing a denial of service.

[67]   The fast reconnect feature improves functionality, not security. Therefore, this claim is considered optional from a security perspective. Nevertheless, organizations that expect their users to change associations frequently may have a strong preference for EAP methods that can make this claim.

Therefore, they can still support IEEE 802.11 RSN associations in the context of other methods that meet the WLAN-required security claims, but these are the only circumstances in which they can be used safely. The RFC 3748 methods are often referred to as legacy methods because more sophisticated EAP methods have been developed since the publication of RFC 3748, but MD5-Challenge in particular remains widely used, particularly in conjunction with other more secure authentication methods. These methods are also used on wired networks, where the eavesdropping threat is believed to be much lower.

6.1.2.1 MD5-Challenge

The MD5-Challenge method is based on the Challenge-Handshake Authentication Protocol (CHAP) defined in RFC 1994.[68] The EAP RFC, RFC 3748, requires implementations to support MD5-Challenge. However, IEEE 802.11i requires the EAP method to support mutual authentication in order to avoid man-in-the-middle attacks. It cites MD5-Challenge as an example of a method that does not meet this requirement.[69]

Like other challenge-response methods, the primary advantage of MD5-Challenge is that passwords are never transmitted in clear text. Instead, the AS provides the STA with challenge text that the STA inputs into the MD5 algorithm along with the password. The resulting MD5 hash value is sent back to the AS, which performs the same operation as the STA. The MD5 algorithm ensures that the AS's hash value will match the response only if the STA has the correct password.

Unfortunately, challenge-response methods are vulnerable to offline dictionary attacks and man-in-the-middle attacks unless they are carefully designed, with sufficient entropy in the challenge, keys of the appropriate length, a strong hash function, and secure protocol design. In the offline dictionary attack, the attacker captures both the challenge and the response and then iteratively cycles through the entries in a dictionary of likely passwords, inputting the challenge and each dictionary entry into the MD5 algorithm to find a match with the response. If the attacker finds a match, the entry that produced the match is the password. In the man-in-the-middle attack, the attacker impersonates the STA to the AS and the AS to the STA. This configuration allows the attacker to get the correct response from the STA without the AS ever knowing that it did not originate from an authorized entity.

To mitigate the risk of dictionary and man-in-the-middle attacks, challenge-response methods such as MD5-Challenge can be tunneled within a method that encrypts the entire challenge-response sequence. In this scenario, the clear text challenge is encrypted, and the encrypted response is encrypted a second time. This approach is a common configuration for WLANs that rely on IEEE 802.1X port-based access control and is designed to help prevent dictionary and man-in-the-middle attacks. Unfortunately, the method used to establish the encrypted tunnel may itself be vulnerable to a man-in-the-middle attack, unless the tunnel establishment employs a method based on mutual authentication. If such an attack is successful, then the encrypted tunnel no longer hides information from the adversary because the adversary established the tunnel in performing the attack and has the keys necessary to encrypt and decrypt EAP traffic. Organizations should be aware that it is not possible to eliminate completely the risk of successful dictionary or man-in-the-middle attacks for challenge-response methods.

---

[68] For more information on CHAP, see RFC 1994, *PPP Challenge Handshake Authentication Protocol (CHAP)* at http://www.ietf.org/rfc/rfc1994.txt

[69] The Wi-Fi Alliance requires EAP-TLS to attain Wi-Fi certification. Therefore, most IEEE 802.11 implementations include support for EAP-TLS.

6.1.2.2   One-Time Password (OTP)

The OTP method, which is based on RFC 2289 and RFC 2243,[70] involves the use of an identical OTP generator on the peer and authenticator. The generator iterates a secure hash function a specified number of times using a passphrase and random seed as the initial input. After each successful authentication transaction, the number of iterations is reduced by one, resulting in a unique series of passwords. The OTP generator can reside on a hardware token or in software on a client computer (e.g., a STA). The OTP method cannot make any of the WLAN required security claims, but potentially could be used if it were tunneled within another method that can support the required claims.

6.1.2.3   Generic Token Card (GTC)

The GTC method is used for hardware token schemes that require user input. The EAP Request contains a displayable message, and the EAP Response contains the token-generated information needed for authentication. Like MD5-Challenge and OTP, GTC does not support any of the required WLAN security claims, but could be used if it were tunneled within another method that can support the required claims.

6.1.3   TLS-Based EAP Methods

The EAP methods defined in RFC 3748 have a number of serious security shortcomings; one of the most significant is that they do not generate key material. Without key material, the WLAN software on the STA and AP cannot apply protections to the traffic between STA and AP, as required for WLAN security. Consequently, IEEE 802.11 RSN solutions must deploy EAP methods other than those defined in RFC 3748 for the networks to be operational, regardless of the level of security desired. RFC 3748 states that due to the complexity of developing key generation algorithms, EAP methods should be based on well-established and analyzed key establishment and generation techniques. In practice, this recommendation limits potential methods to those based on the following key establishment and generation protocol: Transport Layer Security (TLS),[71] a revision of Secure Sockets Layer (SSL), which is most commonly used to secure Web site communications.

TLS has emerged as the dominant protocol for EAP methods that support IEEE 802.11 RSNs. TLS can use public key certificates for authentication and secure transfer of key material; it also supports authentication via pre-shared keys.[72] TLS is designed either to authenticate a server to a client or to mutually authenticate the client and server to each other. For a device to be authenticated using TLS, it must host a public key certificate or be provisioned with a pre-shared key. In an IEEE 802.11 RSN context, if TLS using certificates is used only to authenticate the AS and generate key material, then only the AS must possess a certificate. In addition, the STA needs to have a copy of the AS's certificate in order to authenticate the AS. In this scenario, the AS must authenticate the STA using one or more additional EAP methods tunneled within the TLS session. However, if TLS with certificates is used for mutual authentication, then both the STA and the AS must have certificates. Mutual TLS authentication generally is more secure than one-way TLS authentication coupled with one or more additional EAP methods.

---

[70]   For more information, see RFC 2289, *A One-Time Password System*, at http://www.ietf.org/rfc/rfc2289.txt, and RFC 2243, *OTP Extended Responses*, at http://www.ietf.org/rfc/rfc2243.txt

[71]   For more information on TLS, see RFC 2246, *The TLS Protocol, Version 1.0*, at http://www.ietf.org/rfc/rfc2246.txt Another good source of information is NIST SP 800-52, *Guidelines for the Selection and Use of Transport Layer Security (TLS) Implementations*, available at http://csrc.nist.gov/publications/nistpubs/800-52/SP800-52.pdf

[72]   IPsec's IKE has always included authentication using pre-shared secret keys The TLS Working Group recently adopted RFC 4279, *Pre-Shared Key Ciphersuites for TLS,* to enable both pre-shared key authentication and key derivation

The four most commonly used TLS-based EAP methods are as follows:

- EAP-TLS[73]

- EAP Tunneled TLS (EAP-TTLS)[74]

- Protected EAP (PEAP)[75]

- EAP Flexible Authentication via Secure Tunneling (EAP-FAST).[76]

These methods are described in Sections 6.1.3.1 through 6.1.3.4.

6.1.3.1 EAP-TLS

EAP-TLS is defined in RFC 2716, which was published in October 1999. EAP-TLS is considered the most secure of the widely supported EAP methods, because it allows strong mutual cryptographic authentication of both STA and AS using public key certificates. It is also favored by high-security environments because it is not a compound method, unlike PEAP or EAP-TTLS, and therefore does not suffer from compound binding problems. To enable mutual authentication, each STA must obtain and host its own unique certificate. To provide each STA with its own certificate, organizations should maintain a public key infrastructure (PKI). Ideally, the certificate should be stored on a smart card or other device that can be removed from the STA, but certificates can also be stored on a STA's hard disk or firmware. Use of the certificate should force the user to enter a personal identification number (PIN), password, or passphrase. Otherwise, theft of the STA or card may be all that is needed to authenticate to the WLAN.

Establishing and maintaining a PKI and a smart card infrastructure are not simple endeavors for most organizations. Implemented properly, a PKI involves a certificate policy and practice statement, certificate and registration authorities, and the maintenance of certificate revocation lists, which are needed for denying access when users' devices are stolen or users no longer have a business need to access the network.[77] Accordingly, EAP-TLS might be viable only for organizations that already have a robust PKI in place or are planning one as part of an enterprise identity management solution. Another concern with using EAP-TLS is that its authentication process involves more steps than other methods, so its authentication transactions are slower. This can be problematic in environments in which users are highly mobile, because users might need to re-authenticate frequently and could be frustrated if performance suffers as a result.

Figure 6-1 shows a hypothetical WLAN that uses the EAP-TLS method for authentication. Certificates are located on all of the STAs and the AS. In an infrastructure with several thousand STAs and only several ASs, the need for client certificates greatly increases the level of PKI support required.

---

[73] For more information on EAP-TLS, see RFC 2716, *PPP EAP TLS Authentication Protocol*, at http://www.ietf org/rfc/rfc2716 txt

[74] For more information on EAP-TTLS, see the draft proposed standard, *EAP Tunneled TLS Authentication Protocol Version 1*, dated March 2006, at http://www ietf org/internet-drafts/draft-funk-eap-ttls-v1-xx txt

[75] At the current time, PEAP is not standardized in an IETF RFC or Internet Draft, but expired Internet Drafts describing PEAP are still available

[76] For more information on EAP-FAST, see the draft *Flexible Authentication via Secure Tunneling EAP Method (EAP-FAST)*, dated April 25, 2005, at http://www ietf org/internet-drafts/draft-cam-winget-eap-fast-xx txt

[77] PKI implementations require a considerable investment in time and resources It is outside the scope of this document to discuss PKI in detail See NIST SP 800-32, *Introduction to Public Key Technology and the Federal PKI Infrastructure*, for more information; it is available at http://csrc nist gov/publications/nistpubs/800-32/sp800-32 pdf Another document that might be helpful is *The DoD Public Key Infrastructure and Public Key-Enabling Frequently Asked Questions* Although the document focuses on the Department of Defense PKI, its descriptions of PKI components are applicable to other environments The document is located at http://iase disa mil/pki/faq-pki-pke-may-2004 doc

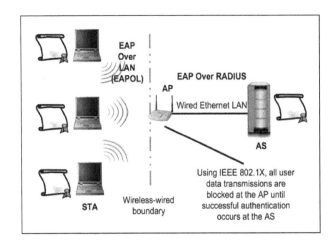

Figure 6-1. Illustration of EAP-TLS Environment

Several WLAN vendors support EAP-TLS in their STA software. Microsoft also supports a version of EAP-TLS in its Windows XP operating system.

6.1.3.2 EAP-TTLS

EAP-TTLS extends EAP-TLS to allow for one-way TLS authentication in addition to mutual TLS authentication. When one-way authentication is used, the AS is authenticated to the STA in a TLS handshake, which also creates an encrypted tunnel between the STA and AS. The tunnel is then used to protect a second authentication transaction in which the STA is authenticated to the AS. In EAP-TTLS, this second transaction is called an *inner authentication method* and occurs in what are termed InnerApplication messages. These messages consist of a series of attribute-value pairs (AVP) that describe the inner application and specify the standard protocols and algorithms that support it. The AVP format is compatible with RADIUS, thereby enabling easy integration with existing authentication protocols that RADIUS supports. The AVP format is extensible, allowing new inner applications and corresponding AVPs to be defined as needed. Currently supported inner applications include EAP methods, CHAP,[78] and PAP. When the inner application is another EAP method, it is referred to as the *inner EAP method.*

The use of EAP-TTLS is similar to Web sites that establish a protected channel, and then prompt for a username and password. The client computer first uses TLS to validate the Web server's certificate and establish an encrypted session with the server. At that point, passwords sent to the Web server are encrypted and therefore protected from eavesdropping. EAP-TTLS operates in a similar manner; the STA validates the AS's certificate and uses the resulting TLS session to transfer user credentials securely.

Figure 6-2 shows a hypothetical WLAN that uses the EAP-TTLS method for authentication. The configuration is identical to the EAP-TLS example in Figure 6-1, but in this case a certificate is present on the AS only.

---

[78] EAP-TTLS also supports the Microsoft variants of CHAP, namely MS-CHAP and MS-CHAPv2. CHAP and MS-CHAP are considered insecure, but MS-CHAPv2 provides adequate security for medium assurance applications. It also supports PAP, which is not secure if used on its own. However, in combination with the outer TLS tunnel, it may be adequate with substantial network engineering devoted to its security.

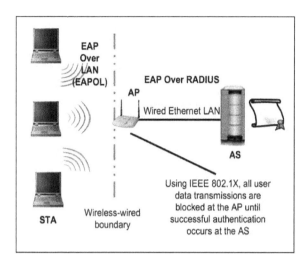

Figure 6-2. Illustration of EAP-TTLS Environment

An advantage of EAP-TTLS relative to EAP-TLS is that it can support legacy authentication methods, using them as the inner authentication method. For example, if an organization has mature security processes and a large investment in an existing identity management system based on passwords, tokens, or biometrics, then it might make sense to leverage that system for its WLANs. It might appear that eliminating the requirement for certificates on STAs (the clients) greatly reduces the administrative complexity of the required supporting PKI; installing certificates on a small number of ASs is considerably easier than installing them on hundreds or thousands of computers or smart cards. However, the root certificate must be delivered securely to every client to prevent man-in-the-middle attacks. Many desktop operating systems include system management tools for the distribution of root certificates to clients. Alternatively, root certificate distribution can be accomplished by the IT department when configuring computers for end users.

The TLS tunnel protects the inner application from several attack types, including replay attacks and dictionary attacks. Unfortunately, it does not always offer strong assurance against man-in-the-middle attacks. Another shortcoming of EAP-TTLS is that it is only as strong as the inner application authentication method that occurs within the TLS tunnel. For instance, if EAP-TTLS is used with a legacy system that allows weak passwords, then that implementation of EAP-TTLS is weak, which in turn means the IEEE 802.1X port-based access control that relies on that implementation of EAP-TTLS is weak. In a cascading fashion, the strength of nearly all elements' RSN protections is rooted in the strength of the EAP-TTLS inner application to authenticate the STA, which is left unspecified. Therefore, organizations that implement EAP-TTLS should carefully consider the risks associated with any candidate method before deploying it.

6.1.3.3 PEAP

PEAP is the product of a joint development effort by engineers from Microsoft, Cisco Systems, and Extundo. PEAP's characteristics are very similar to EAP-TTLS. Like EAP-TTLS, PEAP uses certificates and leverages TLS only to verify the AS's identity to the STA and establish a secure communications channel to protect the transaction in which the STA authenticates to the AS. As with EAP-TTLS, no client certificates are required; however, provisioning the root certificate on each and every client is a mandatory security requirement.

The main difference between EAP-TTLS and PEAP is that PEAP's tunneled authentication transaction is another EAP method rather than an exchange of AVPs. These tunneled EAP methods, also called *inner EAP methods*, might be an RFC 3748 method or a more recently developed EAP method. In practice, this distinction usually is not important because both EAP-TTLS and PEAP can run on any network topology or protocol, are compatible with RADIUS, and can interoperate with any AP, none of which require method-specific code.

Given the similarities between EAP-TTLS and PEAP, it is possible that one will emerge as a de facto standard while the other becomes superfluous, but it is unclear which is more likely to become the standard at this time. A number of vendors are implementing EAP-TTLS in their WLAN products, and EAP-TTLS client software is available for most major operating systems (e.g., Linux, Mac OS, Microsoft Windows). PEAP has strong support from both Microsoft and Cisco Systems, which could encourage other vendors to implement PEAP in their solutions. In addition, Microsoft Windows XP provides native support for PEAP, but not EAP-TTLS. Organizations that require EAP-TTLS for Windows XP STAs need to procure third-party software; an open-source EAP-TTLS plug-in is available for the native Windows supplicant. Also, the Windows version of PEAP supports MS-CHAPv2 only, which currently limits its use to authentication with Microsoft domains or Active Directory. Organizations that need PEAP to interoperate with third-party ASs need to procure compatible third-party PEAP client software. Unfortunately, there are different non-interoperable implementations of PEAP, so organizations should take care that their server and client versions are compatible; they must also be compatible with the method used to store user accounts on the backend authentication database. Both versions should also fulfill the organization's security requirements.

New industry developments could change the relative merits of each method. Neither EAP-TTLS nor PEAP has been approved as an IETF standard; EAP-TTLS is defined in an Internet-Draft, but the PEAP Internet Draft has expired. Given the rapid changes in this area, organizations are encouraged to obtain the latest information before selecting one of these methods.

6.1.3.4 EAP-FAST

EAP-FAST was developed by Cisco Systems. What distinguishes EAP-FAST from other TLS-based methods is that it establishes the encrypted tunnel using what it calls a Protected Access Credential (PAC), which is effectively a pre-shared key; alternatively, a public key certificate can be used. The tunnel is then used to protect an inner EAP method, much like PEAP.[79] The use of PACs eliminates the need to have certificates on either the STA or AS. The protocol also includes mechanisms for refreshing PACs after a successful authentication. EAP-FAST is especially suitable for unsophisticated devices that might not have the computing power to perform TLS handshakes frequently without adversely impacting the user's experience. For example, EAP-FAST might enable household appliances, vending machines, and other small devices not typically connected to WLANs today to participate in IEEE 802.11 RSNs more cheaply and efficiently than they could with other EAP methods.

The major problem with EAP-FAST is initializing each STA with its first PAC. Provisioning initial PACs is not easier than provisioning certificates. Cisco has implemented features on its WLAN equipment that can provision PACs securely, but they involve having a digital certificate on the AS, which must be installed on each client before it can be used. Given these limitations, EAP-FAST in practice has similar PKI requirements to EAP-TTLS and PEAP, even if the certificates are not used in the EAP conversation itself. The alternative, easier method of PAC provisioning, does not require

---

[79] Unlike PEAP and TTLS, EAP-FAST prevents man-in-the-middle attacks through the cryptographic binding of the tunnel and the inner EAP methods

certificates, but is also not secure. Currently, Cisco is the only vendor supporting EAP-FAST, but it might gain wider appeal if it becomes an official IETF standard.

6.1.4 Summary of EAP Methods and Security Claims

Table 6-2 reviews the security claims of each of the EAP methods discussed in Sections 6.1.2 and 6.1.3. None of the RFC 3748 EAP methods can make any of the relevant security claims, but these methods can serve as an inner EAP method when tunneled inside one of the TLS methods.

Table 6-2. Summary of Security Claims for Selected EAP Methods

Security Claim	EAP Method						
	RFC 3748 Methods			TLS-Based Methods			
	MD5	OTP	GTC	EAP-TLS	EAP-TTLS	PEAP	EAP-FAST
Key derivation	No	No	No	Yes	Yes	Yes	Yes
Key strength	N/A	N/A	N/A	Yes	Yes	Variable	Yes
Mutual authentication	No	No	No	Yes	Depends on implemen-tation	Depends on implemen-tation	Yes
Shared state equivalence[80]	No	No	No	Yes	Yes	Yes	Yes
Dictionary attack resistance	No	N/A	No	Yes	Yes	Yes	Yes
Man-in-the-middle attack resistance[81]	No	No[82]	No	Yes	Depends on implemen-tation[83]	Depends on implemen-tation[84]	Yes
Protected ciphersuite negotiation	No	No	No	Yes	Yes	Yes	Yes
Fragmentation	No	No	No	Yes	Yes	Yes	Yes
Confidentiality[85]	No	No	No	Yes	Yes	Yes	Yes
Channel binding	No	No	No	N/A[86]	Optional	Depends on implemen-tation	No
Fast reconnect	No	No	No	Depends on implemen-tation	Yes	Yes	Yes

As Table 6-2 shows, the TLS methods provide similar security claims, primarily because TLS protections offer the basis for most of these claims. The main difference between them is the level of PKI support required, which is summarized in Table 6-3. Also, EAP-FAST can be configured to use non-certificate-based shared secrets such as pre-shared keys. Another difference between the methods is the level of

---

[80] This claim is not defined in RFC 3748, Section 7 2 1, but appears as a mandatory requirement in [STANLEY]

[81] Man-in-the-middle attack resistance is a combination of several RFC 3748 security claims Table 6-1 has a footnote that contains a more detailed discussion of the various security claims behind man-in-the-middle attack resistance

[82] EAP-OTP offers replay protection only

[83] EAP-TTLSv1 is resistant to man-in-the-middle attacks, but it is currently not widely implemented

[84] PEAPv2 is resistant to man-in-the-middle attacks and includes channel binding, but it is currently not widely implemented

[85] RFC 3748 notes that to make the claim of confidentiality, a method must support identity protection The Internet-Draft RFC *EAP Method Requirements for Wireless LANs* refers to this concept as "end user identity hiding"

[86] EAP-TLS does not require channel binding, since it performs authentication as part of the TLS channel

vendor support they receive. EAP-TTLS and PEAP are emerging as the industry-preferred EAP methods for WLANs. EAP-FAST is currently a Cisco-proprietary approach but could gain a wider following if its Internet Draft progresses to RFC status.

Table 6-3. Characteristics of Common TLS-Based EAP Methods for WLANs

Characteristic	EAP-TLS	EAP-TTLS	PEAP	EAP-FAST
AS Certificate	Required	Required	Required	Optional
STA Certificate	Required	Optional	Optional	None
Tunneled Authentication Protocols	N/A	Any method defined in an attribute-value pair using the RADIUS namespace	EAP	EAP

6.2   Developing an EAP Method Strategy

None of the EAP methods offers the best solution for all environments; the selection of an EAP method depends on several factors, including whether an organization intends to leverage existing enterprise authentication infrastructure for its WLAN authentication transactions. If an existing user database is to be used, the EAP method must be compatible with the format in which user credentials are stored. Nothing in the standards that define RSNs—including IEEE 802.11i, IEEE 802.1X, and EAP—requires that STAs and ASs support more than one EAP method.[87] However, the Wi-Fi Alliance requires EAP-TLS for certification. Some products support more options than others. Accordingly, organizations should thoroughly understand their authentication requirements before designing RSNs and procuring WLAN equipment. They should also be aware of any security policy or infrastructure limitations inherent in the existing authentication infrastructure that they might want to leverage for RSN authentication. For example, if they currently maintain a AAA server that by policy is configured to support either tokens or certificates, but not passwords, then they might seek STAs that can work within those constraints. If a password-based system over EAP is selected, the cryptographic protection of the outer TLS tunnel should be extended as far as possible, preferably all the way to the authentication server, but at least to a trusted secure network. This applies to both TTLS and PEAP. Finally, they may want to conduct a risk assessment of various options of EAP methods before selecting one. Some questions that organizations should address before choosing an EAP method are discussed in Table 6-4.

6.3   EAP Security Considerations

The RSN framework specifies the use of IEEE 802.1X authentication and EAP, but leaves a number of critical security implementation details to the discretion of the organization implementing the framework. Potential problems include an adversary impersonating an AP, capturing wireless authentication traffic as it travels over the network between the AP and AS, and exploiting AS security vulnerabilities. This section discusses some of the risks associated with improper implementations and how to mitigate those risks.

---

[87]   This EAP method, MD5-Challenge, is described in Section 6.1.2.1

Table 6-4. Questions for Identifying an Appropriate EAP Method

Question	Analysis
Does the WLAN solution need to support guest users?	Organizations that want to use WLAN technology to provide connectivity to business partners, customers, and guests need an RSN solution based on an EAP method for which there is nearly universal support across potential clients. This requirement effectively limits the selection of EAP methods to those that are supported natively by Microsoft Windows, given its widespread use. Microsoft Windows (XP or newer) supports PEAP and a native version of EAP-TLS. PEAP provides the best support for guest users because it does not require the presence of a client certificate. However, it does not eliminate the requirement to deploy the root certificate on the client. Also, the guest user's PEAP must be compatible with the organizational server's PEAP, and care should be taken that neither version contains known vulnerabilities. EAP-TTLS provides better support for guest users, since it does not require client certificates, does not have PEAP's version incompatibilities, and EAP-TTLS/PAP can be used with any user authentication database.
Will the WLAN solution support equipment from multiple WLAN vendors?	The greater the interoperability requirement, the greater the need to use a commonly used EAP method such as EAP-TLS, EAP-TTLS or PEAP. Proprietary solutions can commit an organization to a single vendor and can complicate upgrades and migrations.
Does the organization currently have a PKI? Does it issue client certificates?	The presence of a PKI greatly facilitates the use of certificate-based methods that require each STA to have a certificate, such as EAP-TLS. EAP-TLS is thus an attractive option if the PKI issues client certificates. If no PKI is available, then the organization should obtain a server certificate from an external PKI provider or consider secure password-based EAP methods.
Does the organization deploy smart cards and readers?	If a smart card infrastructure is already in place, EAP-TLS generally offers the greatest security. Support for smart card-based EAP-TLS solutions is native to recent versions of Microsoft Windows. Alternatively, the session resumption features of PEAP/EAP-TLS or TTLS/EAP-TLS permit the STA to remain connected when roaming, without having to leave the smart card (i.e. ID badge) in the reader all of the time.
Does the organization have an enterprise identity management system?	If the organization has an enterprise identity management system, then there are probably strong security and cost incentives to leverage that system. The appropriate EAP method to deploy depends on the characteristics of the identity management infrastructure.
Does the organization need to support legacy authentication methods?	If a requirement for a legacy authentication method exists, then this method should be protected in a TLS session, especially if the legacy method sends authentication credentials in clear text. EAP-TTLS, EAP-FAST, and PEAP all provide support for TLS tunneling.
Does the organization need to use an existing user database?	If an existing user database is to be used, the EAP method must be compatible with the format in which user credentials are stored.
Is the organization especially concerned about the overall cost of the solution?	Certificate-based EAP methods are more costly to implement and maintain than password-based methods.
Does the organization require a high assurance WLAN solution?	High assurance solutions should consist of strong two-factor cryptographic authentication. One approach to achieve this requirement is EAP-TLS with certificates on PIN or password-protected smart cards. Another approach is PEAP or EAP-TTLS with Generic Token Card (GTC) or possibly a biometric solution.

6.3.1 Secure STA Configuration

EAP authentication methods such as EAP-TLS, EAP-TTLS, EAP-FAST, and PEAP use certificates to authenticate the AS to the STA. One potential pitfall to this approach is that it enables an adversary to impersonate the WLAN infrastructure if that adversary can present a valid certificate, and if WLAN clients are not configured properly. It is common for a WLAN client to be configured by default to accept certificates signed by any certification authority (CA) for which it has a corresponding CA certificate. In most cases, a variety of third-party CA certificates are already installed on the client. This allows an attacker to impersonate the WLAN infrastructure successfully with an SSID and a valid certificate signed by any of the third-party CAs that the client recognizes. Once the attacker has tricked the client into associating with the bogus AP, it might be able to capture the authentication credentials needed to access the real infrastructure. In this scenario, the security of the RSN is circumvented simply as a result of having multiple CA certificates on the STA, which is a common configuration on many computers.

To prevent this situation, STAs should be configured to authenticate to specific servers only, not just any server with a valid certificate. Ideally, servers should be identified by their fully qualified domain name (e.g., as1.xyzAgency.gov) so that the name listed in the AS's certificate can be compared with the name specified in the STA's configuration. STAs should also be configured to accept certificates only from the CA that signed the server certificates. With these two controls in place, the attacker would either have to breach the CA or get it to provide it a certificate with the same name as the authentication server. Both of these attacks are considerably more difficult to execute successfully than the relatively trivial one described earlier. As an additional security measure, an organization might consider using its own CA rather than that of a third-party vendor, if it does not trust the third party to implement the proper controls. This approach requires installing the organization's CA certificate on each STA.

Figure 6-3 shows an example of certificate restrictions on a computer running Microsoft Windows XP Professional. The computer is configured to use EAP-TLS when connecting to a certain SSID, and to accept server certificates signed by either the Symantec Root CA or the Thawte Personal Basic CA.

Nothing in the IEEE 802.11i specification or related standards requires a configuration like this one, but it is essential when a client authenticates the WLAN infrastructure using certificates. Organizations deploying RSNs should consider carefully the configuration of their STAs before activating a new wireless RSN.

6.3.2 Unprotected Links

The infrastructure supporting an RSN authentication transaction consists of three components: a STA, an AP, and an AS. IEEE 802.11i provides a rigorous approach to securing the communications link between the STA and the AP. IEEE 802.1X port-based access control ensures that entities on the STA-side of the AP cannot reach the AS-side of the AP prior to successful authentication. However, both standards explicitly state that protection of the communications link between the AP and the AS is out of their scope. Therefore, organizations deploying RSNs must focus on this gap to ensure the end-to-end security of the WLAN solution. Figure 6-4 illustrates the problem.

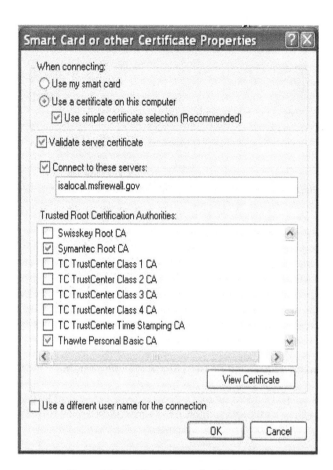

Figure 6-3. Certificate Properties Dialog Box

EAP traffic can be transmitted in the clear between the AP and AS and still not violate IEEE 802.11i specifications. If attackers have access to that communications link, they might be able to view or manipulate traffic in a manner that would allow them to compromise WLAN security. Also, since the key is distributed from the AS to the AP, the key distribution mechanism must be secure. To prevent attackers from viewing or manipulating traffic, organizations should ensure that traffic between the AP and AS is protected sufficiently through cryptography. Ways to accomplish this are as follows:

- Establish a dedicated virtual private network (VPN) between the AP and AS using a VPN protocol such as IPsec.[88]

- Use tunneled EAP methods only, such as EAP-TLS, EAP-TTLS, EAP-FAST, and PEAP.

- Use appropriate key wrapping mechanisms to distribute the key.[89]

---

[88] For additional information on IPsec VPNs, see NIST SP 800-77, *Guide to IPsec VPNs*, available at http://csrc nist gov/publications/nistpubs/800-77/sp800-77 pdf

[89] One example can be found in *RADIUS Attributes for Key Delivery* (http://www ietf org/internet-drafts/draft-zorn-radius-keywrap-xx txt) AES Key Wrap is specified in RFC 3394, *Advanced Encryption Standard (AES) Key Wrap Algorithm*, available at http://www ietf org/rfc/rfc3394 txt

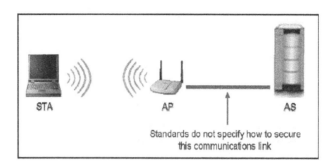

Figure 6-4. Standard IEEE 802.11 RSN Authentication Infrastructure

6.3.3 Attacks on the Authentication Server

Operating system security was not a major concern for pre-RSN WLANs because of the limited functionality of most APs. In an RSN, the core STA authentication function is performed on a separate authentication server, which typically runs on a sophisticated operating system such as UNIX, Linux, or Windows. A breach of the operating system or an application or service with operating system privileges could lead to a complete compromise of RSN security. Accordingly, WLAN security should include hardening of the servers that support the authentication process.[90]

6.4 EAP Multiplexing Model and Related Support Requirements

This section provides additional information on the conceptual architecture of EAP for readers seeking a better understanding of how EAP works and how it interacts with other protocols. Readers who do not need this information should skip this section and proceed to Section 6.5.

RFC 3748 provides a framework for EAP using a four-layer conceptual model described in Table 6-5. It is called the *EAP multiplexing model* because it describes how EAP can handle multiple EAP methods in the same EAP implementation.

Table 6-5. EAP Multiplexing Model

Model Layer	Description
Method Layer	Implements the specified EAP method, which performs the actual authentication transaction. During an EAP dialog, an EAP method on the peer communicates with the equivalent EAP method on the authenticator.
Peer/Authenticator Layer	Forwards EAP packets between the EAP layer and the appropriate EAP method. STAs and ASs that mutually authenticate one another serve in both the peer and authenticator roles. APs serve as pass-through authenticators, proxying traffic for both the STA and the AS when they serve in the authenticator role.
EAP Layer	Manages the EAP dialog—receiving and transmitting EAP packets via the lower layer, detecting duplicate packets, retransmitting packets when necessary, and handling communication with the EAP peer or authenticator. EAP packets containing request, success, or failure notices are delivered to the peer layer; EAP packets containing responses to requests are delivered to the authenticator layer.
Lower Layer	Responsible for encapsulating and transmitting EAP frames between the peer and the authenticator.

---

[90] Checklists and implementation guides for securing various server operating systems are available from NIST's Security Configuration Checklists Program for IT Products at http://checklists.nist.gov/

In a typical IEEE 802.11 RSN configuration, communication flows through the four layers as shown in Figure 6-5. Messages traveling between layers within a device are transported logically within the device's EAP software implementation. Flows between devices occur over a network using lower-layer protocols. Communication flows occur in both directions, as shown by the arrows in the figure. For example, when the EAP method on the AS generates a request, the EAP method on the STA responds to that request. When the AS receives the response, it replies with either a success or failure message, accompanied by key material in the case of success. The Peer/Authenticator layer on each device determines whether to pass the message through (in the case of an AP) or forward it to the appropriate EAP method (in the case of the STA and AS). The EAP layer packages the messages for the lower layer protocols, which are typically IEEE 802.11 or RADIUS.

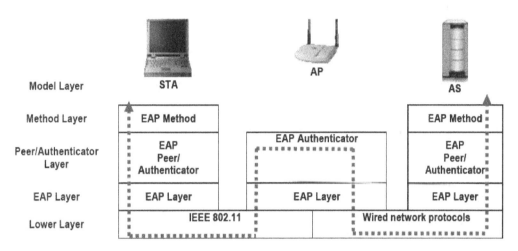

Figure 6-5. EAP Traffic Flow in IEEE 802.11 RSN

EAP implementations differ considerably for the method and lower layers, but are very similar for the middle two layers. Organizations need to determine how to implement the method and lower layers in their environments, which involves selecting one or more EAP methods (discussed previously in Section 6.2) and establishing the protocols that the AS will use to transport authentication messages. Typical support requirements and configurations for each of the key WLAN components are discussed in Table 6-6. The AP does not need to support EAP methods, but it must support the lower layer communications protocols of both the STA and AS.

An important concept at the lower layer is *EAP encapsulation*, which describes how EAP packets are transferred between peer and authenticator. The encapsulation method can differ depending on the network environment. The most common form of EAP encapsulation in IP networks is EAP over RADIUS.[91] In a typical WLAN configuration, the AS either hosts the AAA database or acts as a "front end to the real user database, which might be Active Directory, LDAP, Kerberos, or numerous other alternatives; the AS uses RADIUS to communicate with STAs and other devices. For this reason, the AS is often called the RADIUS or AAA server.

---

[91] For more information on EAP over RADIUS, see RFC 3579, *RADIUS Support for EAP*, at http://www.ietf.org/rfc/rfc3579.txt

Table 6-6. EAP Support Requirements for WLAN Components

Requirement Area	WLAN Component		
	STA	AP	AS
EAP Method Support	Each peer can support multiple EAP methods, but there must be at least one method in common with the AS for a dialog to occur. Supported EAP methods may be native to an operating system or bundled with third-party WLAN software.	The AP does not support EAP methods. It merely passes EAP messages between the STA and AS. Some APs filter EAP methods that they do not allow, although this violates RFC 3748.	The AS is typically a AAA server that supports RADIUS and one or more EAP methods. It can require that the STA use particular EAP methods to authenticate successfully.
Peer/Authenticator Layer Support	The middle layers are implemented in software resident on each of the components of the WLAN solution. Organizations do not have configuration options with respect to the middle layers.		
EAP Layer Support			
Lower Layer Support	The lower layer between the STA and AP is the EAP over LAN (EAPOL) protocol using IEEE 802.11 for media access control and data link communications.	The lower layer between the AP and the AS is likely to be RADIUS over IP. In cases in which the network between the AP and AS is not an IP network, EAPOL using another IEEE 802-series link layer protocol is the most common approach.	

In some implementations, the STA does not have access to IP network services until it successfully authenticates with an AS. When IP services are unavailable, the most common approach is to use EAP over LAN (EAPOL) encapsulation, which enables EAP to be transported in the frames of IEEE 802 link layer protocols. EAPOL is defined in IEEE 802.1X. The WLAN vendor's EAP implementation typically will determine whether the transport mechanism is EAP over RADIUS or EAPOL.

6.5 Summary

Defined in RFC 3748, EAP is used during the authentication phase of an IEEE 802.11 RSN and provides the authentication framework for IEEE 802.11 RSNs that use IEEE 802.1X port-based access control. EAP can be adapted to new authentication methods as they become available and can operate over a variety of different network and link layer protocols, including IP and IEEE 802-series medium access protocols. For these reasons, EAP is well-suited to providing authentication services for WLANs.

EAP defines the stages of an EAP conversation that consists of one or more EAP methods. The EAP methods perform the authentication transaction and generate key material. While the basic rules of the EAP conversation are common to all EAP implementations, the EAP methods can vary from one implementation to another, requiring different levels of user interaction, using different authentication methods, and employing different cipher suites. This flexibility has benefits, but it may also introduce risk. To maintain security, organizations should select EAP methods appropriate to their environment.

IANA has defined numerous EAP method types, but not all of these are appropriate for WLAN applications. For example, RFC 3748 defines three methods—MD5-Challenge, One-Time Password, and Generic Token Card—but none of these can satisfy the necessary security requirements for WLANs.

TLS-based methods such as EAP-TLS, EAP-TTLS, PEAP, and EAP-FAST provide more robust alternatives that can satisfy these requirements. The primary distinction between them is the level of PKI support required. EAP-TLS requires both STAs and ASs to possess valid certificates. EAP-TTLS and PEAP can support configurations with AS certificates only. EAP-FAST can support EAP authentication with certificates or, alternatively, with no certificates, instead using PACs, a type of pre-shared keys. Before organizations select WLAN equipment, they should review their existing identity management infrastructure, authentication requirements, and security policy to determine the EAP method or methods that are most appropriate in their environment, then purchase systems that support the chosen EAP methods.

Many EAP methods are currently defined only in IETF Internet-Drafts and thus are not yet official standards. Organizations are encouraged to obtain the latest available information before making final determinations on their IEEE 802.11 RSN authentication architecture and product procurement.

This page has been left blank intentionally.

7. FIPS and WLAN Product Certifications

Federal agencies are required to use FIPS-approved cryptographic algorithms that are contained in FIPS-validated cryptographic modules. As mentioned in Section 2.1.2, Wi-Fi Protected Access (WPA) and WPA2 are security specifications developed by the Wi-Fi Alliance, a consortium of wireless product vendors that certifies the interoperability of WLAN products through its Wi-Fi CERTIFIED™ testing and branding program. This section describes FIPS 140-2 certification as it applies to 802.11 wireless networks. It also provides an overview of the Wi-Fi Alliance certification programs, with an emphasis on WPA and WPA2. Organizations planning to deploy RSNs should understand the FIPS requirements and the WPA and WPA2 certifications so that they can procure products with the certification levels that best match their WLAN requirements.

7.1 FIPS 140-2 Certification

If a Federal Government wireless network requires security protection, then the data traversing the network must be protected in one of two ways:

- The wireless equipment (APs and STAs) must be FIPS 140-2 certified and must operate in FIPS mode.

- The data on the wireless network must be protected by a VPN. The most common choice is an IPsec VPNs. The VPN's crypto modules must be FIPS 140-2 certified.

In circumstances in which a wired network would not require security protection, a wireless network can also operate without the required security protections. Some examples of this are:

- A wireless network in a conference room that is not connected to either the agency's internal network or to the Internet, which is provided to enable conference participants to communicate with each other.

- A wireless network, connected to the Internet outside of the agency's firewall. Unprotected clients that connect to the wireless network would be able to access the Internet, but accessing the agency's internal network would require security protection.

The above requirements cover protection of the data traversing a wireless network. Authenticating to the network using 802.1X and EAP is somewhat more complicated since EAP standardization is in a state of flux. The IETF's EAP Method Update (emu) working group is working to standardize EAP-TLS and to extend it so that it will meet the needs of today's wireless and other applications but still be backward-compatible with EAP-TLS as defined in RFC 2716. NIST has not standardized on a particular EAP method, so there is no EAP-related FIPS. NIST's Implementation Guidance for FIPS PUB 140-2[92] allows the use of EAP methods based on the TLS protocol (or on SSL v3.1, but not on previous versions of SSL) or on EAP-TLS. Thus, EAP methods that satisfy that requirement and are accepted as secure by the wireless industry may be used by government agencies. Since the RADIUS server is responsible for many of the cryptographic security operations in 802.11i, government agencies are required to purchase RADIUS servers whose crypto modules are FIPS-validated.

---

[92] *Implementation Guidance for FIPS PUB 140-2 and the Cryptographic Module Validation Program* can be found at http://csrc.nist.gov/cryptval/140-1/FIPS1402IG.pdf

7.2 Wi-Fi Alliance Certification Programs

The Wi-Fi Alliance began conducting interoperability testing in April 2000 and has since awarded its Wi-Fi CERTIFIED label to over 2,500 WLAN products. Product categories include access points and a wide variety of clients, including embedded systems, internal and external wireless network interface cards, Universal Serial Bus (USB) devices, and printers. Table 7-1 reviews the three basic types of certifications: radio standards, network security, and multimedia content support. Radio standard certifications involve the electrical engineering aspects of WLAN communications, such as the frequency, power, and modulation of radio signals and the rules by which STAs contend for available channels. The certifications for network security, the subject of this guidance document, cover topics such as authentication and confidentiality services. Multimedia content support refers to quality of service mechanisms that give priority to streaming audio and video over other data, which helps prevent users from experiencing irregular, intermittent multimedia content delivery. To address quality of service interoperability issues, the Wi-Fi Alliance created its Wi-Fi Multimedia (WMM) certification.

Table 7-1. Wi-Fi Alliance Certification Programs

Certification Type	Resulting Certification Label	Underlying Standard
Radio standards	A	IEEE 802.11a
	B	IEEE 802.11b
	G	IEEE 802.11g
Network security	WPA	IEEE 802.11i (subset)
	WPA2	IEEE 802.11i
Multimedia content support	Wi-Fi Multimedia (WMM)	IEEE 802.11e (subset)

All Wi-Fi CERTIFIED™ products must pass interoperability testing with at least one of the radio standards. Otherwise, there would be no assurance that the products could perform their core function of WLAN communications. The network security and multimedia content support certifications supplement the radio standards certification. WPA compliance was initially optional for Wi-Fi CERTIFIED™ products, but was subsequently made mandatory. As of March 1, 2006, WPA2 compliance is mandatory; however, there is a grandfather clause for products that were certified WPA-compliant before that date. Wi-Fi Multimedia (WMM) compliance is likely to remain optional for the foreseeable future.

The Wi-Fi Alliance also manages a licensing program for Wi-Fi providers called Wi-Fi Zone. Organizations participating in the program agree to use Wi-Fi CERTIFIED™ products only and adhere to certain service standards. Customers that see the Wi-Fi Zone logo at an establishment offering Wi-Fi services are offered assurance that they can connect securely and reliably to the Internet. The Wi-Fi Alliance's Web Page (http://certifications.wi-fi.org/wbcs_certified_products.php) contains a search engine that allows viewers to search for various types of wireless equipment that conforms to some or all of its Certification Programs.

7.3 Wi-Fi Alliance Network Security Certifications

WPA and WPA2 are the network security certifications offered by the Wi-Fi Alliance. This section describes these certifications and highlights their differences. It also explains the different certification levels available for both WPA and WPA2: Personal, which uses a pre-shared key for authentication; and Enterprise, which certifies the use of EAP authentication in addition to pre-shared key.

7.3.1 WPA Features

The Wi-Fi Alliance introduced WPA in early 2003 to address serious vulnerabilities inherent in WEP, which was the only available IEEE 802.11 security protection at that time. WPA is a subset[93] of IEEE 802.11i that provides a solution to WEP's major problems. To accomplish this protection, WPA leverages the following core security features from IEEE 802.11i:

- IEEE 802.1X and EAP authentication

- Key generation and distribution based on the IEEE 802.11i 4-Way Handshake

- TKIP mechanisms including

  - Encapsulation and decapsulation

  - Replay protection

  - Michael MIC integrity protection.

Table 7-2 summarizes the primary features provided by IEEE 802.11i that are not included in the WPA test criteria. Organizations that have deployed WPA-compliant equipment can still support IEEE 802.11i RSNs based on TKIP; however, organizations need to determine if the absence of the features not present in WPA is acceptable in their environment. For government organizations, where FIPS compliance is required, this is not acceptable.

Table 7-2. IEEE 802.11i Features Not Present in WPA

Feature	Discussion
IBSS support	WPA does not cover RSN peer-to-peer relationships (i.e., those without APs), also known as ad hoc mode, but this configuration is not common in most enterprises.
Secure fast[94] handoff (through Pre-Authentication and PMKSA caching)	This capability allows users to move from one BSS to another without having to go through the entire authentication process each time. Organizations whose users are expected to migrate between various BSSs frequently (e.g., more than once an hour) may require secure fast handoff to avoid a situation in which users demand a weakening of security requirements to improve performance when they are mobile.
AES-CCMP encapsulation	WPA does not require support for AES-CCMP because the AES-related portions of 802.11i were not sufficiently specified when WPA was released. In most cases, pre-WPA products can achieve WPA-level security with a software upgrade. However, organizations that require FIPS-validated encryption need to procure WLAN products that use FIPS-validated AES-CCMP modules.

7.3.2 WPA2 Features

Released in September 2004, WPA2 is the Wi-Fi Alliance's interoperability certification program for the complete ratified version of IEEE 802.11i. If a product holds the WPA2 certification, it complies completely with the IEEE 802.11 standard as amended by IEEE 802.11i and should work seamlessly with other WPA2-certified products under most operating conditions. Also, WPA2 is backward compatible

---

[93] There are some subtle differences between the TKIP in WPA and in IEEE 802 11i, and the 4-Way Handshake The WPA suites are also identified by a different OUI than the IEEE 802 11i suites

[94] In reality, Pre-Authentication and PMKSA caching are not considered to provide a sufficiently fast handoff to support layer 2 mobility; this was one of the motivations for creating the IEEE 802 11r Task Group, Fast Roaming/Fast BSS Transition

ESTABLISHING WIRELESS ROBUST SECURITY NETWORKS: A GUIDE TO IEEE 802.11i

with WPA, so any WPA2 product should be able to interoperate with a WPA product.[95] Some products may require a hardware upgrade to achieve WPA2 compliance; older products, in general, cannot be upgraded to WPA2.

WPA2 testing validates interoperability with selected EAP methods only, so WPA2 certification does not imply interoperability with all possible EAP methods. Currently, certification involves interoperability testing with the following EAP methods:

- EAP-TLS

- EAP-TTLS/MSCHAPv2

- PEAPv0/EAP-MSCHAPv2

- PEAPv1/EAP-GTC

- EAP Subscriber Identity Module (EAP-SIM).

When a method is listed with a "/", the first term is the actual EAP method, and the second term is the inner method tunneled within it. The Alliance may add to this list over time. Organizations procuring WPA2 products should either select EAP methods from the tested list or conduct their own interoperability testing on the equipment with their own authentication infrastructures.

WPA2 certification does not currently exist for products providing AS functionality. When the Alliance conducts its interoperability testing, it uses AAA servers running leading implementations of RADIUS and the tested EAP methods, but does not publicize which these are. If an organization selects a AAA server running a different implementation of RADIUS or the chosen EAP method, then there is no guarantee of interoperability. Conducting independent testing in enterprise environments is advised.

Because Federal agencies are required to use encryption algorithms that are FIPS-approved, such as AES, they should procure WPA2 components with FIPS-validated cryptographic modules. WPA equipment is not FIPS-compliant because it utilizes the RC4 algorithm instead of AES. Products can obtain WPA2 certification without being FIPS-validated, so Federal agencies should check for both WPA2 certification and FIPS validation.

7.3.3 Modes of Operation

Both WPA and WPA2 have two modes of operation: Personal and Enterprise. The Personal mode involves the use of a pre-shared key for authentication, while the Enterprise mode uses IEEE 802.1X and EAP for this purpose. Products can be certified for both modes or for Personal mode only. Therefore, organizations that plan to use an authentication server rather than pre-shared keys should look specifically for the Enterprise certification. The use of an authentication server rather than pre-shared keys is recommended for most situations because of the impracticality of generating, deploying, and periodically replacing pre-shared keys. The lack of individual user/client authentication in most PSK APs is another reason to avoid the use of pre-shared keys.

7.4 Summary

Federal agencies are required to use FIPS-approved cryptographic algorithms that are contained in FIPS-validated cryptographic modules. In addition, the Wi-Fi Alliance has established several certification

---

[95] WPA2 products implement both WPA and WPA2 (IEEE 802 11i) TKIP and 4-Way Handshakes

7-4

programs to give consumers of WLAN products assurance that their systems comply with IEEE 802.11 specifications and can interoperate with similar equipment from other vendors. The following certifications have been created to test interoperability of IEEE 802.11i implementations:

■ WPA, which addresses a subset of the IEEE 802.11i specification that addresses the weaknesses of WEP

■ WPA2, which extends WPA to include the full set of IEEE 802.11i requirements.

Federal agencies should procure WPA2 products that have been FIPS-validated; WPA products cannot be FIPS-validated because they do not support FIPS-approved encryption algorithms. WPA and WPA2 have both Personal and Enterprise modes of operation. Organizations that plan to deploy authentication servers as part of an IEEE 802.1X and EAP implementation should procure products with the Enterprise level certification; government organizations should also require FIPS conformance or NIST approval.

This page has been left blank intentionally.

8.   WLAN Security Best Practices

As explained in the previous sections, IEEE 802.11 RSNs are complex, involving multiple devices, protocols, and standards. This section distills this complexity into a manageable and actionable set of recommendations that organizations can implement to provide reasonable assurance that they are protected against most WLAN security threats. The recommendations should be particularly helpful to organizations that have made a decision to integrate WLAN technology into their computer networks and want to determine the best way to do it. The recommendations should also be helpful to organizations that are already managing WLANs, but are not satisfied with the level of security they provide; they might want to upgrade, replace, and configure their infrastructure so that it is capable of supporting RSNs and other security controls.

To be effective, WLAN security should be incorporated throughout the entire life cycle of WLAN solutions, involving everything from policy to operations. This section references a five-phase life cycle model to help organizations determine at what point in their WLAN deployments a recommended best practice might be relevant. The model is based on one introduced in NIST SP 800-64, *Security Considerations in the Information System Development Life Cycle.*[96] Organizations may follow a project management methodology or life cycle model that does not directly map to the phases in the model presented here, but the types of tasks in the methodology and their sequencing are probably similar. The phases of the life cycle are as follows:

■ **Phase 1: Initiation**. This phase includes the tasks that an organization should perform before it starts to design its WLAN solution. These include providing an overall vision for how the WLAN would support the mission of the organization, creating a high-level strategy for the WLAN's implementation, developing a WLAN use policy, and specifying business and functional requirements for the solution.

■ **Phase 2: Acquisition/Development.** For the purposes of this guide, the Acquisition/Development phase is split into the following two phases:

— **Phase 2a: Planning and Design**. In this phase, WLAN network architects specify the technical characteristics of the WLAN solution and related network components. These characteristics include the EAP method or methods used to support authentication; the protocols used to support communication between AP and AS; access control lists and firewall rules to segregate WLAN traffic; and the nature of the supporting PKI. The types of clients to be deployed also need to be considered, since they can affect the desired security policies. There is a wide variety of supplicants that may or may not support desired EAP methods; care must be taken to ensure that the security policy can be employed and enforced by all components (client, AP, and AS). A site survey is typically conducted to help determine the number and placement of access points, as well as how they integrate into the existing network.

— **Phase 2b: Procurement**. This phase involves specifying the number and type of WLAN components that must be purchased, the feature sets they must support, and any certifications they must hold.

■ **Phase 3: Implementation**. In this phase, procured equipment is first configured to meet operational and security requirements, and then installed and activated on a production network. Implementation includes altering the configuration of other security controls and technologies, such as security event logging, network management, AAA server integration, and PKI.

---

[96]   This document is available at http://csrc.nist.gov/publications/nistpubs/800-64/NIST-SP800-64.pdf

- **Phase 4: Operations/Maintenance**. This phase includes security-related tasks that an organization should perform on an ongoing basis once the WLAN is operational, including log review and rogue AP detection.

- **Phase 5: Disposition.** This phase encompasses tasks that occur after a system or its components have been retired, including preserving information to meet legal requirements, sanitizing media, and disposing of equipment properly.

The recommendations presented in this section are provided in tables corresponding to the life cycle phases. Each recommendation is accompanied by a brief explanation of the rationale for its inclusion, and is rated as "best practice" or "should consider". Organizations are strongly encouraged to adopt the "best practice" recommendations. Failure to implement them significantly increases the risk of a WLAN security failure. Organizations should also examine each of the "should consider" recommendations to determine their applicability to the target environment. In general, "should consider" recommendations enhance security beyond what can be achieved through the "best practice" recommendations. A "should consider" recommendation should be rejected only if it is infeasible or the reduction in risk from its implementation does not justify its cost.

Organizations should develop their WLAN security controls based not only on the recommendations in the tables, but also using other guidance on security controls. FIPS Publication (PUB) 199 establishes three security categories—low, moderate, and high—based on the potential impact of a security breach involving a particular system.[97] NIST SP 800-53 provides recommendations for minimum management, operational, and technical security controls for information systems based on the FIPS PUB 199 impact categories.[98] The recommendations in NIST SP 800-53 should be helpful to organizations in identifying controls that are needed to protect networks and systems, which should be used in addition to the specific recommendations for WLANs listed in this document.

Some large organizations divide their IT duties among various teams. For example, one group may be responsible for desktop and laptop support, while another might focus on the network infrastructure. In these organizations, implementation of a WLAN may require participation from multiple IT support teams. To assist with this division of labor, the tables identify the impacted WLAN components (i.e., STA, AP, AS, DS) for each of the listed recommendations. When the DS is listed, it refers to the switches, routers, and network media of the organization's enterprise network behind each AP. In most cases, these are part of a wired network.

The tables can also serve as checklists; the status column on the right is blank so that IT staff can use it to measure progress toward implementation of the recommendations.

---

[97] FIPS PUB 199, *Standards for Security Categorization of Federal Information and Information Systems*, is available at http://csrc nist gov/publications/fips/fips199/FIPS-PUB-199-final pdf

[98] NIST SP 800-53 Revision 1, *Recommended Security Controls for Federal Information Systems*, is available at http://csrc nist gov/publications/nistpubs/800-53-Rev1/800-53-rev1-final-clean-sz pdf

Table 8-1. IEEE 802.11 RSN Security Checklist: Initiation Phase

				Checklist		
#	**Security Recommendation**	**Rationale / Discussion**	**Impacted Components**	**Best Practice**	**Should Consider**	**Status**
		Initiation Phase				
1	Perform a risk assessment to understand WLAN threats, the likelihood that those threats will be realized, and the potential impact of realized threats on the value of the organization's assets.[99]	The risk assessment is an important input to the development of the WLAN usage policy because it iden ifies which WLAN activi ies pose an acceptable risk to the organization's information resources and which do not.	ALL	✓		
2	Establish a WLAN usage policy that specifies which user communities are authorized to use WLAN technology and for what purposes.	A WLAN usage policy is the foundation on which subsequent security controls are based. It should be defined and enforced by WLAN trained staff or consultants. The policy should explicitly identify if WLANs are available to business partners, customers, and other guests. It should also identify the information resources that shall and shall not be available to WLAN users (e.g., allow a guest to use the organiza ion's Internet connec ion but not access its internal database servers). Finally, the policy should describe the terms under which an organization's WLAN-capable mobile devices (e.g., laptops) can be used on external WLANs (e.g., home, hotel, coffee shop).	STA / AP/AS	✓		
3	Require that all connections to an organization's WLANs be based on an IEEE 802.11i RSNA using IEEE 802.1X/EAP authentication.	Sections 3 and 4 detail the reasons why RSN associations are superior to pre-RSN authentication techniques. The RSNAs should be based on IEEE 802.1X/EAP au hentication rather than pre-shared keys. Also, the RSNAs should use CCMP leveraging a FIPS-validated AES encryption module. Organizations may relax this requirement for public-use WLANs if they disclose that those WLANs provide no security for wireless connections; if so, they may require a cap ive portal ("splash page") system to provide users with relevant legal disclosures and disclaimers.	STA	✓		

---

[99] For more information on performing risk assessments, read NIST SP 800-30, *Risk Management Guide for Information Technology Systems* All NIST SPs are available for download from http://csrc nist gov/publications/nistpubs/800-30/sp800-30 pdf

				Checklist		
Initiation Phase						
#	Security Recommendation	Rationale / Discussion	Impacted Components	Best Practice	Should Consider	Status
4	Establish or enhance opera ing system and application security configuration standards for laptops and other potential STAs to account for WLAN risks.[100]	WLAN-capable devices typically are at greater risk of a security breach than wired-only devices and may require additional security controls beyond those already present. The configuration standard should require personal firewall and anti-virus software for all STA platforms for which such security products are commercially available. Remote connectivity to the devices (e.g., file sharing, open network ports) should be limited where feasible.	STA	✓		
5	Establish or enhance opera ing system and application security configuration standards for the AS.	The ASs should be among he most secure servers in the enterprise because a breach of an AS could allow an adversary to access the network without a physical connection, perhaps even beyond the organization's physical perimeter. Special emphasis should be placed on preventing exposure of cryptographic keys to unauthorized parties.	AS	✓		
6	Require that administration and network management of WLAN infrastructure equipment (i.e., APs and ASs) involve strong authentication and encryption of all communication.	IEEE 802.11i does not specify any requirements related to the management and administrative interfaces of WLAN equipment, so it cannot be assumed that these interfaces are secure. If an organization uses Simple Network Management Protocol (SNMP) to manage its equipment, it should use SNMPv3,[101] which has enhanced security features relative to its predecessors. Web-based administra ion should use SSL/TLS or an equivalent protection (e.g., IPsec).[102] Secure shell (ssh) and secure ftp (sftp) can be used for command-line access and file uploads.	AP / AS	✓		

---

[100] NIST has a repository of security configuration checklists for various operating systems and applications, which is located at http://checklists.nist.gov/. The checklists can be helpful to organizations in securing STAs, ASs, and other RSN components. NIST SP 800-70, *Security Configuration Checklists Program for IT Products*, describes the checklist program in more detail

[101] For more information on SNMPv3, see http://www.snmp.com/snmpv3/, which provides links to pertinent RFCs, trade press articles, white papers, and related Web sites

[102] More information on TLS is available from NIST SP 800-52, *Guidelines for the Selection and Use of Transport Layer Security (TLS) Implementations*. Another helpful resource is NIST SP 800-77, *Guide to IPsec VPNs*, which compares IPsec, TLS, and other methods for protecting network traffic

	Initiation Phase					
				Checklist		
#	Security Recommendation	Rationale / Discussion	Impacted Components	Best Practice	Should Consider	Status
7	Educate users about the risks of WLAN technology and how to mitigate those risks.	Security awareness and training helps users to establish good security practices to prevent inadvertent or malicious intrusions into an organization's information systems. WLAN security content should be integrated into existing security awareness programs when feasible. [103]	ALL	✓		
8	If applicable, develop or revise the organization's PKI certificate policy, certification practice statement, and related processes to support the WLAN solution.	The certificate policy and certification practice statement are the foundation of PKI security. An IEEE 802.11i RSN can leverage a PKI if it uses IEEE 802.1X port-based access control with an EAP method based on public key cryptography, which is expected to be the case in nearly all large enterprises that deploy RSNs. A PKI may also be used to support IPsec connections that supplement the RSN solution (e.g., for securing communication between AP and AS, which is not required in WLAN standards). This recommendation is not applicable in environments without a PKI and may not be applicable in environments that use the PKI services of a third party. [104]	STA / AS	✓		
9	Require two-factor authentication for WLAN connectivity. [105]	Two-factor authentication enhances the strength of the authentication procedure, making it less likely that adversaries will successfully exploit it. Two-factor authentication could include use of biometrics or smart cards, which could significantly increase the cost of the WLAN solution. Organizations should weigh the costs and benefits of any proposed authentication solution. For users, devices whose credentials cannot be re-used require re-authentication when roaming from one AP to another; this makes this approach cumbersome and potentially unusable. In cases in which two-factor authentication is determined to be unnecessary for users, it should still be considered for administrative connections to WLAN infrastructure.	STA / AS		✓	

---

[103] NIST SP 800-50, *Building an Information Technology Security Awareness and Training Program*, contains detailed guidance on designing, developing, implementing, and monitoring an IT security awareness and training program

[104] More information on PKI is available from NIST SP 800-32, *Introduction to Public Key Technology and the Federal PKI Infrastructure*

[105] For more guidance on authentication, see NIST SP 800-63, *Electronic Authentication Guideline*

Initiation Phase						
#	Security Recommendation	Rationale / Discussion	Impacted Components	Checklist		
				Best Practice	Should Consider	Status
10	Establish requirements for a WLAN intrusion detection system.[106]	Intrusion detection systems deployed on the wireless network can detect and respond to potential malicious activi ies, including unauthorized WLAN vulnerability scanning and the installation of rogue APs. The results of the risk assessment should help determine he level (if any) of intrusion detection required.	STA / AP / DS	✓		
11	Use the services of security professionals to assist with WLAN security issues if the requisite skill sets are not currently available in the organization.	Wireless security is a complex field. Even small flaws in implementation can have significant ramifications for he resulting security of the WLAN solu ion. Well-trained professionals can help mitigate this risk.	ALL		✓	

---

[106] Section 3 5 3 1 5 of NIST SP 800-48, *Wireless Network Security: 802.11, Bluetooth and Handheld Devices*, provides information on wireless intrusion detection systems and discusses the shortcomings of using intrusion detection systems intended for wired environments in wireless applications   Also, NIST SP 800-94, *Guide to Intrusion Detection and Prevention Systems*, provides information on wireless intrusion detection and prevention systems

Table 8-2. IEEE 802.11 RSN Security Checklist: Planning and Design Phase

				Checklist		
Planning and Design Phase						
#	Security Recommendation	Rationale / Discussion	Impacted Components	Best Practice	Should Consider	Status
12	Conduct a site survey to determine the proper loca ion of APs, given a desired coverage area.	The site survey should result in a report that proposes the location for each AP, graphically notes its usable coverage area, and assigns it an IEEE 802.11 radio channel.[107] The estimated usable range of each AP should not extend beyond he physical boundaries of the facility whenever possible. To best achieve this result, APs should be located near the center of rooms and away from exterior walls and windows. In addition, APs should be located in areas that can be physically secured to prevent unauthorized tampering.[108] Configuring APs to only accept connections at higher data rates helps limit the effective coverage area as well.	AP		✓	
13	Create a dedicated Virtual LAN (VLAN)[109] to support AP connections to he distribution system (e.g., enterprise wired network).	Using dedicated VLANs to support wireless connections to the enterprise network segregates wireless traffic from other network communications. Dedicated VLANs facilitate the use of network access control lists, which identify the protocols and services that are allowed to pass from WLANs to the DS. Different VLANs can be defined within he wireless connections to further separate varying security policies.	AP / DS		✓	

---

[107] The nature of electromagnetic radiation is such that determining the precise boundaries of a WLAN is not feasible Nevertheless, an organization can estimate boundaries for usable coverage ranges based on empirical tests with typical STAs and APs

[108] The core risk associated with lack of AP physical security is that someone might be able to reset the AP to manufacturer defaults, which could disable RSN protections Exactly what needs to be physically secured depends on the characteristics of the AP technology When discussing the concept of an AP, this document assumes that AP security and radio functionality are integrated in the same device In most cases, particularly home and small office applications, this is true However, in some product offerings, a WLAN switch supports the IEEE 802 11i RSN AP security functions of session keys generation, TKIP or CCMP encapsulation and decapsulation, and pass through communication between the STA and AS This switch connects to multiple radio devices, each of which has an antenna and proprietary methods for secure communication with the switch In an IEEE 802 11i RSN, the device requiring physical security is the one that performs the AP security functions When those functions are performed on a WLAN switch, that switch should be in a locked communications closet, server room, or data center When those functions are collocated with the radio, then the radio should be physically secured In many cases, the radios often are placed on conference tables, above ceiling tiles, or in other areas that are easily accessible In these cases, the radio should be placed in a locked box with holes that allow for protruding antennas

[109] A VLAN is a logical group of STAs that communicate as if they were on the same physical LAN, even though they might be on different ones VLANs are created through the configuration of one or more switches across an enterprise

Planning and Design Phase						
#	Security Recommendation	Rationale / Discussion	Impacted Components	Checklist		
				Best Practice	Should Consider	Status
14	Ensure that network management information between APs/ASs and network management servers or consoles is transmitted over a dedicated management VLAN.	This control is applicable only in cases in which APs or ASs can support a dedicated management interface. A dedicated management VLAN can be used to transfer pre-shared keys, execute management commands, and transmit audit data without he risk that non-administrative users can eavesdrop on that communication. Segregating this type of traffic is often referred as out of band communica ion because it occurs over a separate channel than those that support data traffic. Out of band channels are particularly useful during denial of service attacks, when severe congestion on data channels may prevent administrators from implementing corrective security measures if hose data channels are the only ones available to them. This sensitive VLAN traffic should be protected.	AP / AS		✓	
15	If a WLAN will be supporting unau henticated users, such as members of the public, install a network firewall between each WLAN and its distribution system.[110]	A firewall can enforce a security policy on the information flow between the WLAN and its distribution network, allowing only authorized protocols and services to traverse this boundary. Firewalls are necessary if access to the WLAN is extended to users who are not positively iden ified by 802.11i, such as members of the general public.	AP / AS / DS		✓	
16	Install a personal firewall on each mobile device.	A personal firewall can enforce a security policy on he information flow between he STA and other parties, allowing only authorized protocols and services to access the STA. This can prevent direct attacks on he STA before the completion of the 4-Way Handshake; it can also prevent attacks from other clients attached to the same AP after the completion of he 4-Way Handshake.	STA	✓		

---

[110] Guidance on network firewalls is available from NIST SP 800-41, *Guidelines on Firewalls and Firewall Policy*

				Checklist		
#	**Security Recommendation**	**Rationale / Discussion**	**Impacted Components**	**Best Practice**	**Should Consider**	**Status**
		Planning and Design Phase				
17	Develop wireless security audit processes and procedures that identify the types of security relevant events that should be captured, and determine how audit records will be securely stored for subsequent analysis.	Developing a program of audit processes and procedures will help ensure that the organization can detect unauthorized behavior and security breaches on wireless systems. Both APs and ASs should send event data to a secure audit server in real time so that the integrity of previously captured audit data is protected even when the AP or AS is compromised. Events to be captured should include, at a minimum, both successful and unsuccessful authentication and association attempts.	AP / AS	✓		
18	Select an appropriate EAP method or EAP method sequence for WLAN authentication, and design any necessary integration with PKI technology.	EAP method selection is the cornerstone of RSN security protections; a poor EAP implementation can undermine nearly all aspects of RSN security. Appropriate EAP methods are those that meet the required security claims listed in Section 5.1.2. They usually will include one or more of he TLS-based methods (e.g., EAP-TLS, EAP-TTLS, PEAP) because TLS is the preferred method for distributing key material. If the TLS method uses an inner application or method, these should also be identified at this time. All TLS methods require at least some integration with a PKI, even if certificates are required on ASs only. Careful planning of the authentication methods and supporting infrastructure ensures that RSNAs will comply with the organization's security policy and objectives.	STA / AS	✓		
19	Determine the fallback strategy when WLAN authentication fails.	Authorized users sometimes fail to successfully authenticate to the WLAN, even though they have a valid business reason to use the network. Reasons include forgotten passwords and lost smart cards. There should be a fallback strategy to provide access to these users. In some cases, this might involve a human process such as a call to the help desk to reset a password. In other cases, it might involve a technical process, such as providing users the ability to enter a pass phrase when hey are using a STA that does not hold a personal cer ificate. In either situation, the fallback method should be at least as strong as the primary method, otherwise attackers will attempt to exploit the weaker fallback approach.	AS	✓		

Planning and Design Phase						
#	Security Recommendation	Rationale / Discussion	Impacted Components	Checklist		
				Best Practice	Should Consider	Status
20	Deploy wireless intrusion detection systems to detect suspicious or unauthorized activity.	Intrusion detection systems enable the organization's operations or security staff to identify and respond to attacks on the organization's systems or information resources before they inflict the maximum potential damage. The radio coverage of wireless intrusion detection devices should be at least as great as that of the WLANs they are intended to protect. If the coverage area of the intrusion detection system were smaller than the coverage area of the WLAN, then attackers could position themselves to circumvent the intrusion detection system.	STA / AP	✓		

Table 8-3. IEEE 802.11 RSN Security Checklist: Procurement Phase

Procurement Phase						
#	Security Recommendation	Rationale / Discussion	Impacted Components	Checklist		
				Best Practice	Should Consider	Status
21	Procure WPA2-Enterprise certified STA and AP products only.[111]	Only WPA2-Enterprise certified products are capable of fully implementing the IEEE 802.11i RSN protections, including CCMP support and IEEE 802.1X port-based access control.	STA / AP	✓		
22	Procure products that use FIPS-validated cryptographic modules and deploy them in "FIPS mode" if required.[112]	Federal agencies are required to use FIPS-validated cryptographic modules. Cryptographic modules that are not FIPS-validated cannot be assured of providing the level of cryptographic protection intended through use of RSN technology. When reviewing the list of a vendor's FIPS-validated products, organizations should check that the validation is for the algorithms that will be deployed in the organization's RSN (e.g., CCMP).	STA / AP	✓		

[111] For a listing of WPA2-Enterprise and other Wi-Fi Alliance certified WLAN systems, visit https://certifications.wi-fi.org/wbcs_certified_products.php
[112] For a listing of FIPS-validated cryptographic modules, visit http://csrc.nist.gov/cryptval/

				Checklist		
#	**Security Recommendation**	**Rationale / Discussion**	**Impacted Components**	**Best Practice**	**Should Consider**	**Status**
			Procurement Phase			
23	Procure STAs and APs that support NIST AES key wrap with 128-bit HMAC-SHA-1 to protect transient keys during the 4-Way and Group Key Handshakes.	AES provides assurance of key confidentiality, while HMAC-SHA-1 provides assurance of key integrity. Protecting the PTK and GTK during transit is critical to protecting the communications that rely on those keys for data confidentiality and integrity. The alternative algorithm permitted by IEEE 802.11i for the 4-Way and Group Key Handshakes is RC4 encryption (for confidentiality) with HMAC-MD5 (for integrity), but RC4 has known vulnerabilities, and neither algorithm is FIPS-validated.	STA / AP	✓		
24	Procure ASs and APs that communicate in a secure manner.	The communication link between the AS and AP should be secured. The MSK distribution from AS to AP should use appropriate key wrap mechanisms.	AS/AP	✓		
25	Procure products that support the organization's chosen EAP methods.	If the organization invests in products that do not support the chosen EAP methods, then either the equipment cannot be used (resulting in wasted expenditure) or pressure may exist to modify the organization's security configuration to support alternative methods, which might weaken the network security. Both STAs and ASs must support the chosen EAP methods. Organizations should test EAP interoperability between STAs and ASs before final procurement.	STA / AS	✓		
26	Procure APs that terminate associations after a configurable time period.	IEEE 802.11i does not specify the length of time for which an RSN association is valid, potentially allowing WLAN sessions to remain open indefinitely. A session termination feature in the AP would cause STAs to reauthenticate if network access is still needed after a fixed period of idleness or connectivity. While not required by the standard, this functionality mitigates the risk that an adversary could use active RSN associations for unauthorized purposes for an indefinite period of time.	AP	✓		

				Checklist		
		Procurement Phase				
#	Security Recommendation	Rationale / Discussion	Impacted Components	Best Practice	Should Consider	Status
27	Procure ASs that grant authorizations for a configurable time period.	IEEE 802.11i does not specify the length of time for which an RSN association is valid, potentially allowing WLAN sessions to remain open indefinitely. A session termination feature in the AS would cause STAs to reauthenticate if network access is still needed after a fixed period of idleness or connectivity. While not required by the standard, this functionality mitigates the risk that an adversary could use active RSN associations for unauthorized purposes for an indefinite period of time.	AS		✓	
28	Procure APs that log security relevant events and forward them to a remote audit server in real time[113].	Audit technology helps ensure that the organization can detect unauthorized behavior and take actions to prevent or limit the extent of a security breach. IEEE 802.11i does not require a logging capability, so organizations must seek this functionality outside the standards framework. The AP should support the functional audit requirements developed during the planning and design phase. The AP should have a feature to forward events automatically to a central audit server.	AP	✓		
29	Procure APs that can support an independent management interface to the distribution system (e.g., wired network).	Support for an independent management interface enables organizations to establish an out of band channel for key transfer and other administrative functions.	AP		✓	
30	Procure APs that support SNMPv3 if the organization plans SNMP-based AP management.	SNMPv3 has enhanced security features relative to its predecessors.	AP		✓	
31	Procure APs that support authentication and data encryption for administrative sessions.	IEEE 802.11i does not specify security for administrative connections to APs, potentially allowing unauthorized management of these devices if not properly secured. Examples of protections include SSL/TLS support for Web-based administration and secure shell (SSH) for command-line administration.	AP	✓		

---

[113] More information on log management is available from NIST SP 800-92, *Guide to Computer Security Log Management*

#	Security Recommendation	Rationale / Discussion	Impacted Components	Checklist Best Practice	Should Consider	Status
		Procurement Phase				
32	When he WLAN solution involves TLS-based EAP methods, procure STAs whose software can be configured to specify valid ASs by name.	If a STA does not specify the valid servers with which it can authenticate, a potential exists for an adversary to insert a bogus AS into the WLAN infrastructure as part of a man-in-the-middle attack.	STA	✓		
33	Procure APs and ASs that can support IPsec or alternative security methods to establish a mutually authenticated secure communications channel between AP and AS.[114]	IEEE 802.11i and its related standards (IEEE 802.1X, EAP, etc.) assume a preexisting trust relationship between the AP and AS and further assume that the communication between them is secure. If organizations do not implement technology to realize these characteristics, then the assumptions are invalid and RSN security could be compromised. IPsec is the most common means of establishing a secure communications channel between two devices, but equivalent protection can be provided with link layer security controls and other protocols designed to ensure the confidentiality and integrity of network communications.[115]	AP / AS	✓		
34	Procure APs and ASs that support Network Time Protocol (NTP).	NTP allows distributed devices to synchronize timestamps, which is critical to effective log analysis because it allows audit personnel to establish accurate event sequences across multiple devices. In addition, IEEE 802.11i suggests that the nonce in the 4-Way Handshake should be based on NTP time whenever possible. If not, the cryptographic properties of the 4-Way Handshake could be weakened in some circumstances.	AP / AS		✓	
35	Procure an auditing tool to automate the review of AP and AS audit data.	Audit tools often are more effective than humans at distilling relevant information from multiple sources. In large enterprise WLAN deployments, reviewing the amount of data generated could overwhelm technical support staff if they do not have appropriate tools to assist them with this task.	AP / AS / DS	✓		

[114] More information on key management is available from NIST SP 800-77, *Guide to IPsec VPNs*
[115] Potential options include Secure Shell (SSH) and TLS

	Procurement Phase					
#	Security Recommendation	Rationale / Discussion	Impacted Components	Checklist		
				Best Practice	Should Consider	Status
36	Procure products that can be upgraded easily in software or firmware.	WLAN products require this support so that they can take advantage of wireless security patches and enhancements released after original delivery. Not all APs support his feature, so this functionality should be verified before procurement.	ALL	✓		

Table 8-4. IEEE 802.11 RSN Security Checklist: Implementation Phase

	Implementation Phase					
#	Security Recommendation	Rationale / Discussion	Impacted Components	Checklist		
				Best Practice	Should Consider	Status
37	Ensure that all APs have strong, unique administrative passwords.	To protect against dictionary attacks, administrator passwords on APs should be hard to guess. In addition, organizations should not use a common password for multiple APs. Otherwise, a compromised password on one AP could have much wider consequences.	AP	✓		
38	Disable all insecure and unused management protocols on the APs, and configure remaining management protocols for least privilege.	Disabling all insecure and nonessential management protocols eliminates poten ial methods that an adversary can use when attempting to compromise an AP. Examples of insecure management protocols include SNMPv1 and SNMPv2. If SNMPv3 is used, configure it for least privilege (i.e., read only) unless write access is required (e.g., to change configura ion set ings as part of an automated incident response procedure).	AP	✓		
39	Disable WEP and TKIP in the configuration of each AP.	If WEP remains enabled, then STAs might be able to negotiate WEP for authentication and encapsulation, which would negate RSN protections. Similarly, if an organization's security policy requires CCMP, but TKIP remains enabled, then STAs might negotiate TKIP instead of CCMP.[116]	AP	✓		

---

[116] IEEE 802 11i allows for RSNs based on data confidentiality and integrity protocols other than TKIP and CCMP, including vendor proprietary algorithms, as long as they use the 4-Way Handshake for authentication and key distribution These vendor proprietary solutions could have easily exploitable vulnerabilities, which heightens the need to disable unused protocols

				Checklist		
			Implementation Phase			
#	**Security Recommendation**	**Rationale / Discussion**	**Impacted Components**	**Best Practice**	**Should Consider**	**Status**
40	Activate logging and direct log entries to a remote audit server.	Logs enable security and support staff to identify potential security issues and respond accordingly. Using a remote central logging server facilitates reviews of logs across the enterprise and ensures the integrity of log data when he AP or AS is compromised.	AP / AS	✓		
41	Establish an IPsec connection (or equivalent protection mechanism) between each AP and its associated AS or ASs.	The standards assume that the AP and AS have a preexisting trust relationship but never specify how hat relationship is established. A mutual authenticated secure connection between AP and AS must exist to prevent an adversary with access to the distribution system from impersonating the AS or eavesdropping on the transfer of key material among other potential attacks. Exploits of this nature could greatly undermine the efficacy of RSN protections.	AP / AS		✓	
42	Configure a maximum GMK lifetime on the AP, preferably not to exceed 24 hours.	The GMK is used to protect multicast traffic. Setting a maximum GMK lifetime reduces the exposure of data if the GMK is ever compromised.	AP	✓		
43	Configure a maximum PMK lifetime on the AS, preferably not to exceed eight hours.[117]	In the IEEE 802.11i RSN framework, the PMK is used to derive all o her encryption keys used to secure various types of WLAN communication. Setting a maximum life ime for the PMK reduces the probability that an adversary can compromise it.	AS	✓		
44	Configure the STA and AS to use authorized EAP methods only.	If both the STA and AS allow EAP methods other than those permitted in the security architecture, then a potential exists that the STA and AS will use the unauthorized method in a manner hat circumvents the organization's security policy.	STA / AS	✓		
45	When TLS methods are used, ensure hat the STAs connect to valid ASs only.	If a STA connects to an unauthorized AS, that AS will be able to capture authentication credentials and severely compromise network security. To ensure authorized connections, the STA should be configured to specify the names of valid ASs, specify the locally stored CA certificate used to validate the digital signature of the AS certificate, and require that the STA check for AS certificate revocation.	STA	✓		

---

[117] Some organizations may operate mission-critical applications that require real-time responsiveness, and therefore cannot tolerate even small delays associated with rekeying or reauthentication transactions In this relatively rare situation, organizations may wish not to set a PMK lifetime, effectively making it infinite, and make PMK changes during scheduled maintenance downtime

Implementation Phase						
#	Security Recommendation	Rationale / Discussion	Impacted Components	Checklist		
				Best Practice	Should Consider	Status
46	Disable ad hoc mode on each STA unless a business requirement exists for peer-to-peer wireless networking.	Most organizations that deploy WLANs use infrastructure mode only, in which STAs connect to an enterprise network through APs. Attackers can use ad hoc mode to gain access to a computer's information resources with litle effort, particularly when he STA is configured improperly (e.g., default settings have not been changed). The wireless IDS should monitor the use of ad hoc mode on the wireless network. Organizations that require ad hoc mode should develop and apply a standard configuration to each STA and develop procedures for implementing and replacing pre-shared keys.	STA	✓		

Table 8-5. IEEE 802.11 RSN Security Checklist: Operations/Maintenance Phase

Operations/Maintenance Phase						
#	Security Recommendation	Rationale / Discussion	Impacted Components	Checklist		
				Best Practice	Should Consider	Status
47	Test and deploy software patches and upgrades on a regular basis.[118]	Newly discovered security vulnerabilities of vendor products should be patched to prevent inadvertent and malicious exploits. Patches should also be tested before implementation to ensure that they work properly.	ALL	✓		
48	Ensure that all passwords are changed regularly.	Passwords should be changed regularly to reduce he risk of a compromised password being misused; it may be possible to configure the user management system to enforce password updates.	ALL	✓		
49	Review audit logs frequently.	Frequent reviews of audit logs allow security and support personnel to iden ify security issues and take corrective or preventative measures quickly. All components of the WLAN solution should generate event logs, especially the AP and AS. Automated logging tools can assist with log review and send real-time alerts in response to critical events. Events to track include failed authentication attempts and MIC failures.	AP / AS / DS (STA optional)	✓		

---

[118] More information on patching is available from NIST SP 800-40 version 2, *Creating a Patch and Vulnerability Management Program*

				Checklist		
Operations/Maintenance Phase						
#	Security Recommendation	Rationale / Discussion	Impacted Components	Best Practice	Should Consider	Status
50	Inventory APs.	A complete inventory of an organization's authorized APs is the basis for iden ifying rogue APs during security audits and can be helpful for a variety of support tasks.	AP	✓		
51	Inventory STAs.	STAs have the potential to provide an adversary with an entry point into the enterprise network, par icularly if a user has ac ivated ad hoc mode, which allows peer-to-peer connections from other STAs. Understanding where STAs are located and how they are used can assist with risk assessments, audits, and other support tasks. Taking an inventory of STAs is most practical in organizations that already have mature asset management systems.	STA	✓		
52	Perform comprehensive WLAN security assessments at regular and random intervals.	Security assessments, or audits, are an essential tool for checking the security posture of a WLAN and identifying corrective actions necessary to maintain acceptable levels of security. WLAN security assessments should include radio detection of rogue APs; verification of STA, AP and AS configura ion settings; and review of audit logs.	AP / AS	✓		
53	Re-apply the organization's security configuration standard to an AP whenever its reset func ion is used.	Security settings typically are returned to factory defaults after a reset event, which usually occurs when an AP experiences an operational failure. Appropriate personnel need to restore the standard security configuration to ensure that RSN protections are maintained whenever a reset occurs.	AP	✓		
54	If an organization uses PSKs to establish RSN associations, replace them frequently, preferably at least every 30 days.	Most organizations do not require PSKs, relying instead on the alternative key management techniques integrated with various EAP methods. Organiza ions that distribute pre-shared keys, either manually or through proprietary automated solutions, need to replace he keys periodically to reduce the risk that hey will be compromised.[119]	STA / AP	✓		
55	If PSKs are used to establish RSN associations, ensure that no key is shared across multiple STAs.	Ensuring the uniqueness of each PSK limits the impact of a key compromise on communica ions between he STA and AP that hold he key. If any STA/AP combination shares a PSK with another STA/AP combination, a STA or AP in one pair could compromise the communica ion of the other pair.	STA / AP		✓	

---

[119] More information on key management is available from NIST SP 800-57, *Recommendation on Key Management*

Operations/Maintenance Phase						
				Checklist		
#	Security Recommendation	Rationale / Discussion	Impacted Components	Best Practice	Should Consider	Status
56	Periodically update the certificates on the clients and the servers.	This is especially important on client devices, which must have accurate root and intermediate CA certificates loaded locally in order to be able to authen icate the AS correctly.	STA / AP		✓	
57	Designate an individual or group to track WLAN product vulnerabilities and wireless security trends.	Assigning responsibility to an individual for tracking wireless security issues helps ensure continued secure implementation of the organiza ion's WLANs.	ALL	✓		

Table 8-6. IEEE 802.11 RSN Security Checklist: Disposition Phase

Disposition Phase						
				Checklist		
#	Security Recommendation	Rationale / Discussion	Impacted Components	Best Practice	Should Consider	Status
57	When disposing of a WLAN component, remove all sensitive configuration information, including pre-shared keys and passwords.	Adversaries can use sensitive information on discarded devices to conduct subsequent attacks on the organization's networks. Organizations should use degauss devices when feasible.[120] Disk wiping utilities can be used for devices that have hard disks. Another option is to clear configuration settings manually using the management interface.	ALL	✓		

---

[120] Degaussing is a technique in which a powerful magnetic field is applied to an electronic storage device to erase permanently any stored data

				Checklist		
#	Security Recommendation	Rationale / Discussion	Impacted Components	Best Practice	Should Consider	Status

Disposition Phase

#	Security Recommendation	Rationale / Discussion	Impacted Components	Best Practice	Should Consider	Status
58	When disposing of a WLAN component, ensure that its audit records are retained as needed to meet legal or other requirements.	Information contained in the audit records may be needed even after the WLAN component is discarded (e.g., for an investigation of a subsequently discovered security breach). Organizations should identify the legal requirements to retain records that apply to their operations.[121] When log events are forwarded to a central audit server, as is recommended, regular backup of the server facilitates the retention of records. When a log server does not exist, the disposal process needs to include capturing the existing log data and storing it on alternative media, such as CD-ROM or tape.	ALL	✓		

---

[121] An example of a requirements document is General Records Schedule (GRS) 24, *Information Technology Operations and Management Records* GRS 24 is available from the National Archives and Records Administration at http://www.archives.gov/records-mgmt/ardor/grs24.html

This page has been left blank intentionally.

9. Case Studies

This section presents three case studies to illustrate how various issues discussed in Sections 3 through 8 might be addressed in practice. Although the case studies are hypothetical, they are intended to resemble real-world problems and solutions. They do not cover all the aspects of system engineering or all the technical implementation details that an organization should consider when implementing an IEEE 802.11 RSN; they provide a representative sample of the issues an organization may face. The case studies are as follows:

- **Case Study 1: First Time WLAN Deployment.** This case study presents the scenario of an organization that planned to deploy a WLAN for the first time. With no existing WLAN infrastructure to replace or update, the organization methodically applied the best practices introduced in this guide.

- **Case Study 2: Transitioning an Existing WLAN Infrastructure to RSN Technology.** This case study discusses an organization that had implemented WLAN technology already but later wanted to migrate to a RSN framework. Having just experienced a major WLAN security breach, the organization felt that it must act quickly. To meet its needs, the organization developed and implemented first an interim WLAN solution, and then a long-term one.

- **Case Study 3: Supporting Users Who Are Not Employees.** This case study presents the scenario of an organization that planned a future WLAN deployment, whose WLAN user population will consist of many people who are not employees, or perhaps may not have any prior relationship with the organization. It created a security architecture that allows for access from a very diverse set of users. Supporting these users might not require an IEEE 802.11 RSN.

In each case study, the organization followed the information system development life cycle introduced in NIST SP 800-64, *Security Considerations in the Information System Development Life Cycle,* and the best practices discussed in Section 8.

9.1 Case Study 1: First Time WLAN Deployment

For several months, many of agency XYZ's employees had requested the ability to read e-mail and access Web sites when they were in the agency's conference rooms. Several technically inclined users had suggested that a WLAN solution could provide this functionality more effectively than wired connectivity. The agency's IT group initially resisted implementation of WLAN technology, citing security concerns such as the vulnerabilities of WEP. These concerns were allayed substantially with the final release of IEEE 802.11i and its RSN framework. Additionally, the IT group knew they could now identify interoperable IEEE 802.11i-compliant products through the Wi-Fi Alliance's WPA2-Enterprise product certification program. Given these developments, the agency's CIO commissioned an enterprise WLAN deployment project in conjunction with other agency executives. The agency used the NIST SP 800-64 information system development life cycle model to guide the project, but excluded the disposition phase because it would not occur until some time after the project had been completed.

9.1.1 Phase 1: Initiation

The first step in the project plan was to conduct a risk assessment that identified agency information assets and the threats a new WLAN could pose to those assets. The assessment's conclusion was that the mission of the agency could be significantly impacted if external users were able to access the agency's internal network, and that a WLAN solution would need to provide reasonable protection against such threats.

The second step in the project plan was to bring together the major stakeholders to draft a WLAN use policy and gather functional requirements for the WLAN solution. The stakeholder advisory panel agreed that the WLAN would be for the use of employees and full-time on-site contractors only; other users should be prevented from using the WLAN through the implementation of user authentication and authorization technology. The panel also wanted users to be able to roam to any conference room in the building without having to reconfigure their laptops or other wireless devices. Finally, the panel requested that users be able to access all information resources available from their wired desktops, including Internet access. The WLAN use policy also specified who is authorized to install APs (e.g. not end users), as well as which techniques would be used to detect and handle rogue APs.

An attorney on the panel noted that the agency's memorandum of understanding (MOU) with several state governments explicitly prohibited the agency from using wireless networks to access sensitive information that the state governments enter into a database system that the agency calls StateConnect. A network engineer from the IT group had argued that this limitation was unnecessary because RSN protections offered a better defense against eavesdropping and data modification than the agency's wired networks. Nevertheless, the panel eventually agreed that the MOUs would need to be honored regardless of the assurance an RSN could provide. The solution would have to include technical controls to prevent WLAN users from accessing any portion of the StateConnect database system. However, the panel agreed that MOUs should be updated in the next revision cycle to account for advances in WLAN security.

9.1.2 Phase 2: Acquisition/Development

With the WLAN use policy and a solid set of functional requirements in place, the IT staff started the acquisition/development phase of the project. The first step was a site survey to help determine the network architecture of the WLAN solution. All 20 conference rooms were located in the center of the building, which meant the risk of radio emanations beyond the property's perimeter was unlikely. Testing established that installing one AP in each conference room would provide adequate coverage for all except the two large conference rooms on the ground floor, which would require three APs to provide adequate connectivity. Testing also confirmed that WLAN emissions would be contained within the building. The resulting plan called for mounting the APs in the center of each conference room, immediately above the ceiling tiles.

The design team wanted to segregate the APs from other network components to improve security and manageability. Unfortunately, the conference rooms were too far apart from each other to connect all of the APs to a dedicated WLAN hub or switch. Accordingly, in the network design, each AP was cabled to the nearest available switch, which typically reside in communications closets near each conference room. The switches were configured to place each port supporting an AP on a single enterprise VLAN. The VLAN spanned the entire building and behaved as if all the APs were on a single local network segment, thereby providing the desired isolation from the rest of the network. The VLAN was connected to the rest of the agency's network through a router. To prevent WLAN users from reaching the StateConnect database, the plan specified an access control list (ACL) on the router that prohibited all traffic from any device on the WLAN to any servers supporting the database and vice versa.

Everyone on the project team quickly agreed that RSN authentication should be based on IEEE 802.1X port-based access control rather than pre-shared keys, primarily because the administrative burden of managing pre-shared keys would likely overwhelm the IT support staff and the fact that PSK does not always uniquely authenticate the end node. On the other hand, determining which EAP method to use with IEEE 802.1X generated more debate. Several technicians wanted to implement the WLAN as quickly and painlessly as possible. They wanted to use the wireless client support bundled with the operating system common to all of the agency's client computers. Then they argued that the logon servers (called domain controllers) supporting file, print, and messaging services should also serve as the ASs in the WLAN solution. This proposal suggested the use of PEAP with MS-CHAPv2 as the inner method. MS-CHAPv2 is a challenge-response method with characteristics similar to MD5-Challenge but with better security.

Unlike the IT support staff, the project manager and information security officer emphasized security over administrative convenience. They wanted authentication to involve a client PKI certificate. The agency was planning to deploy an enterprise PKI in six weeks, which would involve certificates on all agency-owned computers, including desktops, laptops, handheld devices, and servers. The WLAN project was an excellent application for the new PKI and would quickly demonstrate its value. The decision was made to integrate the WLAN with the PKI, which would cause a short project delay, but one that was believed well worth the slip in the schedule. This approach led to the decision that EAP-TLS would be the best choice. Fortunately, the existing domain controllers could also serve as the ASs for the WLAN in this configuration, so the IT support staff accepted this element of the design.

Once the project team completed the design documentation, the next step was to procure equipment. The results of the site survey demonstrated a need for 24 enterprise APs (three for each of the large conference rooms, and 18 for the remaining conference rooms). Based on the selected design, no need existed for additional WLAN client software, switches, or AS infrastructure beyond what was already in-house. The agency sought APs that were WPA2-Enterprise certified and FIPS-validated for the AES encryption module used in the CCMP data confidentiality and integrity protocol. The agency also wanted a means for physically securing the reset button on the APs to help prevent tampering. The search resulted in two candidates, until a member of the project team realized that one of the two products was FIPS-validated for the IPsec AES implementation on its wired interface, but not for the CCMP implementation on its wireless interface. This attention to detail was critical in identifying appropriate WLAN components.

A member of the team created a network design diagram to help guide the subsequent implementation process. The result of that effort is presented in Figure 9-1.

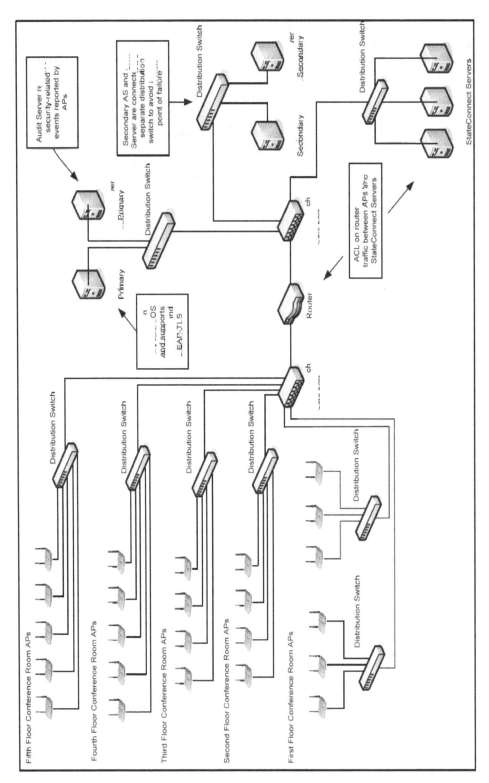

Figure 9-1. Agency XYZ WLAN

9.1.3 Phase 3: Implementation

When the APs arrived, the IT group was just completing its PKI rollout. Each of the APs was similarly configured with the following:

- A common SSID to support roaming across the enterprise

- IEEE 802.1X pass-through, enabling the ASs to perform authentication transactions

- Disabling WEP and TKIP to prevent connections using a data confidentiality and integrity protocol other than CCMP

- IPsec tunnels with each AS to protect authentication and key distribution traffic on the wired network

- Forwarding of AP-generated security events to the enterprise audit server for analysis and real-time intrusion detection.

Each client computer (or STA) was updated with new configuration settings using a combination of logon scripts and enterprise management software. The configuration was relatively complex, requiring that the STA specify the following:

- The SSID of the agency's enterprise WLAN

- The use of IEEE 802.1X port-based access control

- EAP-TLS as the authentication method

- The names of each AS that could perform the authentication transaction

- The CA certificate used to verify the AS certificate's digital signature

- The client certificate used to authenticate the STA to the AS.

The secure configuration is invoked for the SSID of the enterprise WLAN only. Each user can still configure additional SSIDs for connections to hotspots at hotels, conferences, and elsewhere. Personal firewall software on each laptop ensures that other hotspot users cannot gain unauthorized access. The laptop also automatically launches VPN client software for remote connections to the enterprise network, which may be occurring over insecure wireless links.

Finally, technicians configured each domain controller to serve as an AS by doing the following:

- Ensuring that the server was hardened against possible attack, which included installing all current patches as required by vulnerability management policy, and reviewing the system's configuration against the organization's security policies and server security configuration baseline

- Establishing IPsec connections with each AP to protect authentication and key distribution traffic on the wired network

- Forcing use of EAP-TLS to support WLAN authentication.

Before users were allowed to use the WLAN, they were required to complete a 20-minute, Web-based WLAN security awareness course. The course covered important aspects of the WLAN use policy, including not letting people other than employees and full-time on-site contractors use the WLAN, and not accessing the StateConnect database over the WLAN. The course also provided several tips and tricks regarding how to protect one's computer when using non-agency WLANs, such as those found at home, hotels, and coffee shops. For example, users were instructed to verify that their personal firewall software was running and their antivirus and anti-spyware software was up-to-date whenever they used their computers outside of the office. Without this type of protection, data stored locally on an agency laptop could be compromised if the laptop were used on an external network. Also, users could inadvertently download viruses, spyware, and other malware that otherwise would have been blocked by the agency's network-based security controls.

9.1.4 Phase 4: Operations/Maintenance

Security was also integrated into regular operations behind the scenes. Personnel in the agency's Network Operations Center were trained on how to respond to security alerts issued by the log analysis tool on the audit server that received data from each of the APs. Also, on a random day of each month, a technician would walk through the entire building using a laptop-based detection tool to identify unauthorized wireless services (APs and clients), rogue devices, and interfering devices intruding on the IEEE 802.11 channels. The agency was considering the procurement of a wireless intrusion detection system that can identify such devices automatically, but the budget did not allow for such a system in the initial deployment.

9.1.5 Summary and Evaluation

Six months after the deployment of the WLAN, the project team received a special service award from the director of the agency. When announcing the award, the director noted the project management approach to integrating WLANs into the agency's existing IT services. Stakeholders were involved early in the process, and the solution was driven by clearly defined policy and functional requirements. The procurement process led to the selection of appropriate equipment that met all security requirements. Both users and support staff received relevant training related to the new system. The introduction of the IEEE 802.11 RSN at agency XYZ was a huge success.

9.2 Case Study 2: Transitioning an Existing WLAN Infrastructure to RSN Technology

A few days after the new CIO arrived at the Bureau of Advanced Research (BAR), she was confronted with a serious security breach: an intruder had compromised a key database containing confidential business information, and then posted sensitive records on a Web server in a country that did not cooperate with U.S. law enforcement. The preliminary investigation traced the attack back to an unsecured AP that the Special Projects Division had installed for the use of its staff. The AP was placed next to a window and was clearly visible from the public parking lot below. Apparently an unauthorized party had exploited WLAN vulnerabilities and gained access to confidential data. In this situation, little hope existed of finding the perpetrator.

The CIO knew that the bureau's WLAN infrastructure needed a security upgrade immediately to prevent further breaches of bureau information systems. She read about IEEE 802.11 RSNs in the trade press and believed that this could be the solution to the bureau's problem. One of her biggest challenges would be overcoming the fiercely skeptical nature of the bureau's senior scientists, over whom she had little authority. Many of them worried that a centralized security solution would compromise their independence and unnecessarily restrict their scientific pursuits. The CIO had to make the transition as smooth as possible to avoid criticism that could undermine her future success.

The team agreed that the need for immediate security coupled with the diversity of equipment and configurations meant that an upgrade could not happen in one step; there would need to be an interim solution before they could upgrade to the end state.

9.2.1 Phase 1: Initiation

The first step was to inventory the existing WLAN infrastructure, which had grown without a cohesive plan or tight configuration management. A survey found that computers with WLAN client software could support TKIP (although few were using it), while only a few could support CCMP. The IT department managed four ESSs and two BSSs collectively supported by 14 APs with varying capabilities and security configurations. The ESS that supported the IT department used a RADIUS-based AAA server for authentication based on smart cards with PKI certificates. The smart card solution also provided physical access control for the server room and logical access control for several network management consoles. Figure 9-2 depicts the network prior to the migration. Table 9-1 lists a summary of the AP inventory for Figure 9-2.

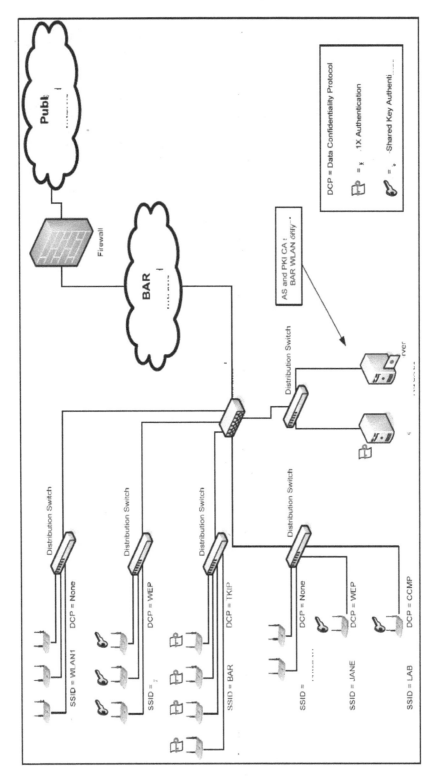

Figure 9-2. BAR WLAN Infrastructure Prior to Transition Effort

Table 9-1. BAR WLAN Components Prior to Transition Effort

AP	BSS/ESS SSID	Existing Data Confidentiality Protocol	Existing Authentication	Wi-Fi Alliance Network Security Certification	Supported Users
1	WLAN1	None	Open	None	Biomedical
2	WLAN1	None	Open	None	Biomedical
3	WLAN1	None	Open	WPA2-Enterprise	Biomedical
4	GC	WEP	PSK	WPA-Personal	General Counsel
5	GC	WEP	PSK	WPA-Personal	General Counsel
6	GC	WEP	PSK	WPA-Enterprise	General Counsel
7	BAR	TKIP	IEEE 802.1X with EAP-TLS	WPA-Enterprise	IT Support
8	BAR	TKIP	IEEE 802.1X with EAP-TLS	WPA-Enterprise	IT Support
9	BAR	TKIP	IEEE 802.1X with EAP-TLS	WPA2-Enterprise	IT Support
10	BAR	TKIP	IEEE 802.1X with EAP-TLS	WPA2-Enterprise	IT Support
11	PROJECT	None	Open	WPA-Personal	Special Projects
12	PROJECT	None	Open	WPA-Personal	Special Projects
13	JANE	WEP	PSK	None	Media Center
14	LAB	CCMP	PSK	WPA2-Personal	Chemistry Lab

The CIO put together a tiger team of top support professionals and a customer advocate who was very familiar with the technical requirements and politics of each office in the bureau. The team began by establishing a long-term vision for the BAR WLAN: an RSN using IEEE 802.1X port-based access control and CCMP for data confidentiality and integrity. The team agreed that the need for immediate security coupled with the diversity of equipment and configurations meant that an upgrade could not happen in one step; it would be evolutionary. There would need to be an interim solution before they could upgrade to the desired configuration.

The team drafted a WLAN use policy that was approved by the bureau's Change Management Board soon thereafter. The policy stated that WLAN communication within the bureau's network would be based on RSNAs only. Authentication would, at a minimum, be based on a user name and password, although pre-shared key authentication would be permitted for an interim period of 120 days. Those requiring WLAN support not based on RSNAs would be required to operate in a perimeter network separated from the main network by a firewall. The WLAN would be limited to users who possessed valid badges to the facility, including visiting scholars, interns, and contractors. Finally, the WLAN could be used for any business activity also permitted on the wired network.

9.2.2 The Interim Solution: Acquisition/Development and Implementation

To plan the transition, the team decided to develop the interim strategy for each BSS or ESS in the current infrastructure. Factors they considered included the functional capability of the current equipment, the extent to which impacted users were familiar with WLAN key management, and the willingness of the impacted users to accept change. They also consulted several NIST publications to guide them in their planning effort, including NIST SP 800-53, *Recommended Security Controls for Federal Information Systems*. The result of their strategy session was a matrix similar to Table 9-2.

Table 9-2. Interim WLAN Strategy for BAR

BSS/ESS SSID	"As Is" Assessment	Interim "To Be" Solution	Long-Term Considerations
WLAN1	- No security - AP1 and AP2 must be replaced because they do not support upgrades - AP3 can be used in long-term solution because of WPA2-Enterprise certification - Users insist on continued use of WLAN regardless of security posture - AP placed near window	- Place ESS on perimeter network outside the firewall - Require users to use client VPN software to access internal network resources - AP placed near the center of the cubicle area, away from windows and walls	- Move ESS back to internal network once newly procured WPA2-Enterprise equipment is in place - Use password synchronization or single sign-on technology to reduce users' concerns over burden of new security measures - Disallow TKIP
GC	- WEP provides inadequate security - All equipment can support TKIP but not CCMP - AP4 and AP5 cannot support IEEE 802.1X solution because WPA-Personal equipment uses PSK approach only - Users already comfortable with use of PSKs because they are deployed in existing WEP configuration	- Configure APs to use TKIP with PSKs - Establish a temporary Transition Security Network (TSN) that permits both WEP and TKIP associations - Help users to transition to TKIP - Once it is verified that all STAs are using TKIP, remove WEP support to establish an RSN - TSN should be operational for as short a period as possible, preferably no more than 72 hours	- Procure new WPA2-Enterprise APs to support long-term solution - Disallow TKIP
BAR	- ESS is already an RSN using IEEE 802.1X - RSN is based on TKIP, not CCMP, which is required in the long-term solution - AP7 and AP8 are not able to support CCMP and need to be replaced - Smart cards provide high level of authentication assurance	- Keep as is	- Replace AP7 and AP8 with new WPA2-Enterprise APs - Continue to support smart cards in long-term solution if feasible - Disallow TKIP

BSS/ESS SSID	"As Is" Assessment	Interim "To Be" Solution	Long-Term Considerations
PROJECT	- No security - APs can support TKIP, but not IEEE 802.1X or CCMP - Users unfamiliar with PSKs but are receptive to security enhancements, especially since their ESS was the source of the major breach	- Configure APs and STAs to use TKIP with PSKs - Familiarize users with new technology	- Replace AP11 and AP12 with new WPA2-Enterprise APs - Disallow TKIP
JANE	- WEP provides inadequate security - AP13 could support TKIP with a firmware flash upgrade - Users already comfortable with use of PSKs because they are deployed in existing WEP configuration	- Upgrade software to code that supports WPA Personal	- Replace WPA2-Personal AP with new WPA2-Enterprise AP - Disallow TKIP
LAB	- ESS is already an RSN using CCMP with PSK - AP cannot support IEEE 802.1X	- Keep as is	- Replace WPA2-Personal AP with new WPA2-Enterprise AP - Disallow TKIP

In conjunction with the changes, the upgraded BSSs were consolidated into a new ESS with the SSID INTERIM, which used TKIP with PSKs. Since the WLAN1 ESS could not be upgraded immediately, it was migrated outside of the internal network. The BAR and LAB WLANs remained "as is" because they both already met interim security requirements.

The interim solution allowed the project team to quickly implement reasonable security measures without interrupting service or purchasing new equipment or software, while moving towards the long-term high assurance solution. Once they implemented the interim changes, the WLAN infrastructure appeared as depicted in Figure 9-3. The specifications of each AP in the interim infrastructure are listed in Table 9-3.

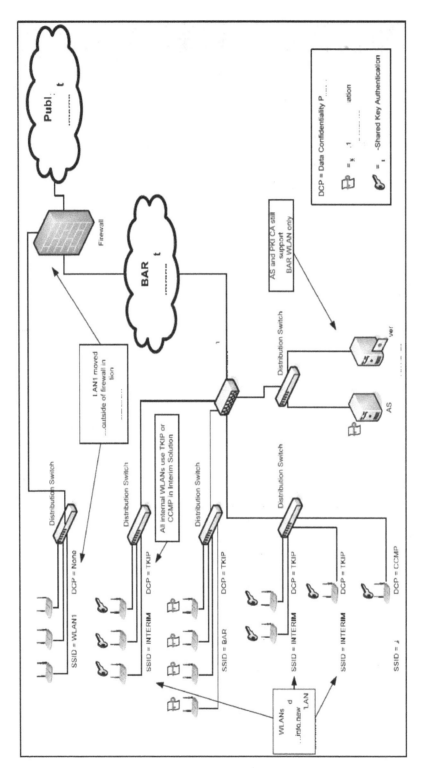

Figure 9-3. BAR WLAN Interim Solution

Table 9-3. AP Specifications in BAR WLAN Interim Solution

AP	BSS/ESS SSID	Interim Data Confidentiality Protocol	Interim Authentication	Wi-Fi Alliance Network Security Certification	Supported Users
1	WLAN1	None	Open	None	Biomedical
2	WLAN1	None	Open	None	Biomedical
3	WLAN1	None	Open	WPA2-Enterprise	Biomedical
4	INTERIM	TKIP	PSK	WPA-Personal	General Counsel
5	INTERIM	TKIP	PSK	WPA-Personal	General Counsel
6	INTERIM	TKIP	PSK	WPA-Enterprise	General Counsel
7	BAR	TKIP	IEEE 802.1X with EAP-TLS	WPA-Enterprise	IT Support
8	BAR	TKIP	IEEE 802.1X with EAP-TLS	WPA-Enterprise	IT Support
9	BAR	TKIP	IEEE 802.1X with EAP-TLS	WPA2-Enterprise	IT Support
10	BAR	TKIP	IEEE 802.1X with EAP-TLS	WPA2-Enterprise	IT Support
11	INTERIM	TKIP	PSK	WPA-Personal	Special Projects
12	INTERIM	TKIP	PSK	WPA-Personal	Special Projects
13	INTERIM	TKIP	PSK	WPA-Personal	Media Center
14	LAB	CCMP	PSK	WPA2-Personal	Chemistry Lab

9.2.3 The Long-term Solution: Acquisition/Development and Implementation

With the interim solution in place, the next stage of the project was to move from the interim solution to the long-term solution. There were three major challenges, as follows:

- Migrate to a centralized authentication infrastructure

- Replace all the APs that were not WPA2-Enterprise certified and therefore could not support CCMP with IEEE 802.1X port-based access control

- Install common client software on all STAs.

With regard to the first challenge, the team was divided as to the approach, with advocates for each of the following proposals:

- Procure a proprietary security policy and key management solution

- Expand the EAP-TLS smart card solution to the entire bureau

- Use the existing RADIUS-based AAA server with EAP-TTLS and MD5-Challenge as the inner EAP method.

The proprietary solution involved agent software on each STA that would periodically obtain a new PSK from a central management server. Proponents of this approach stated that establishing RSNAs based on PSKs was much faster than doing so with IEEE 802.1X and EAP. The team heard sales presentations from several vendors and eventually narrowed on a product suite from Acme Networks. Acme's product suite included a number of productivity-enhancing management tools, including graphical displays of the

WLAN topology with real-time statistics on performance problems and outages. However, the proprietary solution was the most expensive of the options and could constrain future upgrade options, which would frustrate some of the bureau's most influential users.

Smart card supporters argued that it was the most secure of the options because it used two-factor authentication. Moreover, the bureau already had hands-on experience with it, having used it for some time to support the IT staff. Members of this group were worried that an enterprise WLAN solution could weaken the security of the IT infrastructure if the IT staff were compelled to give up their smart cards. The disadvantages to this approach were that the user community might reject the smart cards as overly cumbersome, and that the cards added a significant expense to the project and subsequent operations.

The third group felt the authentication infrastructure needed to be as transparent to users as possible to be accepted readily. Users were used to entering a username and password to access their e-mail, so they should be able to remember a similar combination for authentication to the WLAN. They recommended using EAP-TTLS with MD5-Challenge as the inner EAP method. The AAA server could support this configuration and also communicate using Lightweight Directory Access Protocol (LDAP) with the directory server that stored the e-mail security credentials.

The issue was brought before the CIO for resolution. She rejected the proprietary solution because of its cost. She then successfully brokered a compromise between the second and third groups. Users outside of the IT department would authenticate using their e-mail username and password. The IT staff would also use this system, but would continue to use their smart cards for access to the management network. The SSID of the enterprise ESS would be BAR1; the SSID of the ESS for the IT management network would be BAR2. A firewall between the enterprise user network and the IT management network would strictly limit the types of traffic that can flow between the two of them.

The second challenge was to replace all of the APs that could not support IEEE 802.1X and CCMP. To prevent service disruptions, whenever a new AP was installed, it was configured to support both the old WLAN and the new one. Users were given 60 days to migrate to the new WLAN.

The third challenge was to deploy new WLAN client software on each STA. The IT staff was surprised at the diversity of STAs in their environment and knew that finding RSN client support for all of them would be difficult. The STAs included UNIX, Linux, and Windows computers; two types of personal digital assistants (PDA); six printers; and some smart phones with integrated IEEE 802.11g interfaces. The project team identified a software product that could support EAP-TTLS on UNIX, Linux, Windows, and one of the PDA types, but none of the printers or smart phones. Another product was found for the other PDA type; wireless print servers were found to support the printers.

No support was available for the smart phones, which could support WEP only. Despite the commitment to maintain WLAN service for all users, it was decided that the security of the enterprise could not be compromised for the convenience of a handful of users with IEEE 802.11-capable smart phones. These users were told that they would have to find alternative methods of connecting to the WLAN (e.g., using a PDA).

Several of the original APs did not support CCMP and could not be used in the final solution. This equipment was outdated and no longer of value to the organization. Before donating the equipment to a local elementary school, a technician cleared all keys and network addresses from the devices to avoid revealing any information about the bureau's network to external parties.

Figure 9-4 shows how the WLAN infrastructure appeared at the completion of the project. Table 9-4 lists additional configuration information for the APs in the end-state solution. At this point, all of the APs are WPA2-Enterprise certified and are configured to use CCMP and IEEE 802.1X port-based access control.

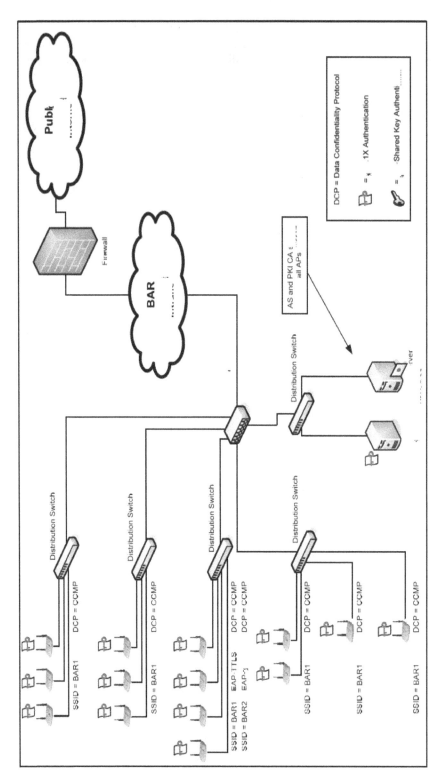

Figure 9-4. BAR WLAN at Completion of RSN Migration Project

Table 9-4. BAR WLAN at Completion of RSN Migration Project

AP	BSS/ESS SSID	Data Confidentiality Protocol	Authentication	Wi-Fi Alliance Network Security Certification	Supported Users
1	BAR1	CCMP	IEEE 802.1X with EAP-TTLS	WPA2-Enterprise	Biomedical
2	BAR1	CCMP	IEEE 802.1X with EAP-TTLS	WPA2-Enterprise	
3	BAR1	CCMP	IEEE 802.1X with EAP-TTLS	WPA2-Enterprise	
4	BAR1	CCMP	IEEE 802.1X with EAP-TTLS	WPA2-Enterprise	General Counsel
5	BAR1	CCMP	IEEE 802.1X with EAP-TTLS	WPA2-Enterprise	
6	BAR1	CCMP	IEEE 802.1X with EAP-TTLS	WPA2-Enterprise	
7	BAR1	CCMP	IEEE 802.1X with EAP-TTLS	WPA2-Enterprise	IT Support
	BAR2	CCMP	IEEE 802.1X with EAP-TLS		
8	BAR1	CCMP	IEEE 802.1X with EAP-TTLS	WPA2-Enterprise	
	BAR2	CCMP	IEEE 802.1X with EAP-TLS		
9	BAR1	CCMP	IEEE 802.1X with EAP-TTLS	WPA2-Enterprise	
	BAR2	CCMP	IEEE 802.1X with EAP-TLS		
10	BAR1	CCMP	IEEE 802.1X with EAP-TTLS	WPA2-Enterprise	
	BAR2	CCMP	IEEE 802.1X with EAP-TLS		
11	BAR1	CCMP	IEEE 802.1X with EAP-TTLS	WPA2-Enterprise	Special Projects
12	BAR1	CCMP	IEEE 802.1X with EAP-TTLS	WPA2-Enterprise	
13	BAR1	CCMP	IEEE 802.1X with EAP-TTLS	WPA2-Enterprise	Media Center
14	BAR1	CCMP	IEEE 802.1X with EAP-TTLS	WPA2-Enterprise	Chemistry Lab

9.2.4 Summary and Evaluation

The transition was a great success, in large part because the project team did not try to reach an ideal state in one step. Instead, it developed both interim and long-term solutions. The interim solution was designed to respond quickly to an active threat. Someone had recently seriously compromised network security and could easily have done so again unless immediate measures were taken to provide a defense against a subsequent attack. In this environment, the bureau did not have the time to procure equipment or develop a new authentication infrastructure.

Fortunately, the organization was able to build an interim IEEE 802.11 RSN with existing equipment. In general, the deployment of PSKs significantly increases the administrative complexity of WLAN operations, primarily because of the need to periodically rotate keys, which is often a manual process. However, the use of PSKs in the interim solution enabled the bureau to protect its WLAN communications quickly, giving it the time to design and implement a long-term solution based on a centralized AS and IEEE 802.1X port-based access control.

In the long-term solution, the bureau decided to leverage its existing RADIUS-based AAA server and integrate it with its LDAP-enabled e-mail directory. It also incorporated its existing smart card authentication system for its IT staff, who desired additional security for access to the bureau's management network. This configuration meant the use of EAP-TTLS with MD5-Challenge password-based authentication for the ESS was available to all users, and EAP-TLS authentication was available for the IT support staff with additional authentication requirements.

9.3 Case Study 3: Supporting Users Who Are Not Employees

The General Regulatory Commission (GRC) was proud of the openness of its proceedings and had successfully used technology to improve its accessibility to the public. Last year, it won an award for its Web site that allows remote users to search through electronic records in its online docket. Recently, it decided to use technology to improve the experience of visitors to its headquarters in Washington, D.C. At the top of its list of project ideas was the installation of new WLAN technology.

GRC's Associate CIO for network engineering and operations had been considering deployment of IEEE 802.11 RSN technology, but was not certain it was best-suited for all of GRC's desired applications. He realized that cyber security threats were real and growing. While the commission embraced technology tools that help it to perform its public service mission, senior staff also knew they needed to balance public access and security. A significant security breach could undermine years of trust the commission had built with its stakeholders.

9.3.1 Phase 1: Initiation

The Associate CIO tasked his IT services contractor to develop a high-level strategy for the WLAN project, in particular analyzing what types of security controls were appropriate for its various components. A few days later, the contractor presented some preliminary ideas, which are shown in Table 9-5.

Table 9-5. Proposed WLAN Architecture and Security Strategy

Section of Building	Users	Potential WLAN Applications	Suggested Approach	Rationale / Discussion
Commission Offices	Employees	Mobile access to office productivity tools (e-mail, Internet, etc.)	- APs placed in conference rooms, employee cafeteria, and commissioners' offices - Employees able to access office systems - ESS is IEEE 802.11 RSNs using EAP-TLS and CCMP (SSID GRC-OFFICE)	- Employees seek standard office WLAN capabilities. - Commissioners want wireless capabilities for meetings in their offices.

Section of Building	Users	Potential WLAN Applications	Suggested Approach	Rationale / Discussion
Administrative Law Courts	Attorneys, reporters, experts/ witnesses, employees	Access to: - Court proceedings/ transcripts - Calendaring system - Evidence information repository	- Both employees and non-employees receive PKI-enabled access badges - Non-employee access to court systems is role-based - Employees able to access both court and office systems - Each hearing room has WPA2-Enterprise AP supporting two ESS: 1. SSID GRC-COURT 2. SSID GRC-OFFICE - ESSs are IEEE 802.11 RSNs using EAP-TLS and CCMP	- Lawyers and reporters have already registered credentials with the court. - Court proceedings are significantly expedited when external parties can connect to some of the court's information systems and their own office systems during hearings. - Members of the public do not have access, but this is not a requirement in the hearing room. - Employees need more access than others, and should be able to roam seamlessly from the commission offices to the hearing rooms. - Data communications require security because some sessions of the court are closed to the public and involve confidential business information.
Public Information Resource Center	Scholars, students, reporters, interested citizens, employees, researchers	Access to: - Public Internet - GRC electronic docket - Library holdings database	- Public WLAN placed outside GRC firewall (SSID GRC-PUBLIC) - Open system authentication with no confidentiality - Connection to Internet throughput-limited on each WLAN channel - Firewall and logging solutions help prevent and log abuses	- Issuing authentication credentials to visitors is administratively burdensome. - Protecting the confidentiality of public information has minimal security value. - Internet connectivity improves research productivity, but throughput is limited on each channel to prevent abuse.

The first step in the initial assessment was recognizing that there were essentially three main areas that could benefit from WLAN services:

- The commission offices, in which employees conducted their day-to-day business

- The administrative law courts, in which registered attorneys, reporters, and expert witnesses needed limited access to court information systems and the ability to access their own office servers. Opposing attorneys' traffic should be isolated from each other, to avoid even the appearance of eavesdropping.

■ The Public Information Resource Center, in which the GRC wanted to offer access to the Internet, the GRC electronic docket, and the library holdings database to all visitors.

The security requirements for each of these areas differed from the others. The simplest case was the commission offices. The requirements there were very similar to those of most other organizations whose WLANs served employees only; meeting areas such as conference rooms and the cafeteria should support mobile users, but do so with RSN protections to protect the confidentiality and integrity of GRC information resources.

The administrative law courts had special requirements, necessitating more rapid access to information. Court proceedings often took far longer to complete than one would expect. For example, whenever someone requested information that was not readily available, the lawyers had to request a recess so that a courier could bring relevant data to the court from wherever it might reside. Determining when to restart a hearing was itself a challenge; all the parties involved had to submit forms specifying their availability, which the court's clerk would use to schedule subsequent appearances.

Allowing authorized individuals access to IT systems from within the hearing rooms could greatly reduce these delays. Attorneys could quickly search through the court's archives or evidence information repository to respond to queries. They could also use VPN technology to access information from external sources, such as the offices of their law firms. In addition, they could enter their schedules into the court's calendaring system, so that when proceedings were stopped, the clerk could immediately notify all parties when they would resume. This functionality required network support. WLAN technology could provide that support unobtrusively, while also giving users a degree of mobility within each room.

One possibility was to permit anyone to use the hearing room WLAN since, for the most part, proceedings were public. This configuration was rejected for two reasons. First, proceedings were closed when cases involved sensitive business information, and much of the court's calendar and its evidence information repository also were confidential. Second, the judges felt that public visitors to the court should not be permitted to use the WLAN for anything other than official court business, which would be difficult to control if they could easily access its network. For these reasons, an RSN solution was deemed appropriate for the hearing rooms and the commission offices.

The final area in which a WLAN would be deployed is the GRC's Public Information Resource Center, which was used by the public, ranging from local university students writing term papers to commission staff checking records related to regulatory actions. Librarians in the center noted that many visitors to the center were frustrated by the lack of Internet access. This situation forced them to leave the center to access information from external resources, sometimes necessitating several trips. A WLAN with Internet access could solve this problem while also facilitating access to the center's resources.

The IT security manager was concerned that public users would abuse their free network privileges, either using them to attack the network or simply dominate the available bandwidth to such an extent that it would crowd out other legitimate uses of the network. He argued for RSN protections to prevent this abuse. However, closer examination of the problem revealed that an RSN was unlikely to solve the potential problems he raised. If members of the public were permitted to use the WLAN on the desired walk-in basis, they could cause problems regardless if they did so on an open system or one on which they were given logon credentials to an RSN. Furthermore, because all the center information that would be accessed is publicly available, confidentiality was not an issue. In the case of the Public Information Resource Center, an RSN would add administrative complexity with little or no additional security benefit.

9.3.2   Phase 2: Acquisition/Development

Based on the IT service contractor's initial analysis, the Associate CIO awarded a task to design the WLAN solution, which focuses on the development portion of the acquisition/development phase of the information system development life cycle. The initial planning had indicated that RSN technology could be useful in the commission offices and the administrative law courts, but was unnecessary in the Public Information Resources Center. The design would need to provide different levels of access to the commission's employees, who for the most part needed full access, and the external parties participating in court proceedings, who needed only limited access.

While the solution could accommodate this differentiation using identity management and authorization software only, the architects felt additional network controls would be required to provide a high level of assurance that the system would not be used improperly. Data traffic in the hearing rooms would be segregated from the main office network using a separate ESS with the SSIDs GRC-COURT and GRC-OFFICE. GRC-COURT would support non-employees with GRC business, such as the attorneys participating in GRC hearings. GRC-OFFICE would support employees and have access to both the office network and the hearing room information resources. The APs in the commission offices would support GRC-OFFICE only. The APs in the hearing rooms would support both GRC-COURT and GRC-OFFICE. Both GRC-COURT and GRC-OFFICE would use the same backend cluster of AAA servers for authentication. The system would be designed to work with any WPA2-certified client, but the hearing room would also have a spare open Ethernet connection for the occasional visitor that still encountered interoperability issues.

The commission already had an enterprise PKI. The badges that both employees and non-employees carried to enter the building could hold PKI certificates that could be used for authentication. Certificate readers were already provided to all employees and could be provided to hearing room visitors on an as-needed basis. With a robust PKI already in place, EAP-TLS authentication was a good choice. Using the PKI to support the WLAN required some changes to the commission's certificate policy and certification practice statement, but these were relatively minor (primarily involving adding WLAN components to the list of acceptable users of the PKI) and were implemented quickly.

The ESS supporting the Public Information Resource Center would have the SSID GRC-PUBLIC. Its APs would be on a VLAN outside of GRC's firewall, which would block all inbound access except requests to its electronic docket and library holdings database. The design also called for limiting the network throughput on each WLAN connection to 256 kilobits per second, which would allow individuals to perform external research but prevent them from dominating the Internet connection so that others would not be able to use it. This requirement was met using a proprietary quality of service feature available on the enterprise APs that the bureau procured for this project. The ability to support this limitation was added to the AP procurement requirements list to ensure that it could be implemented in the final solution.

Figure 9-5 illustrates the design for the GRC WLAN infrastructure.

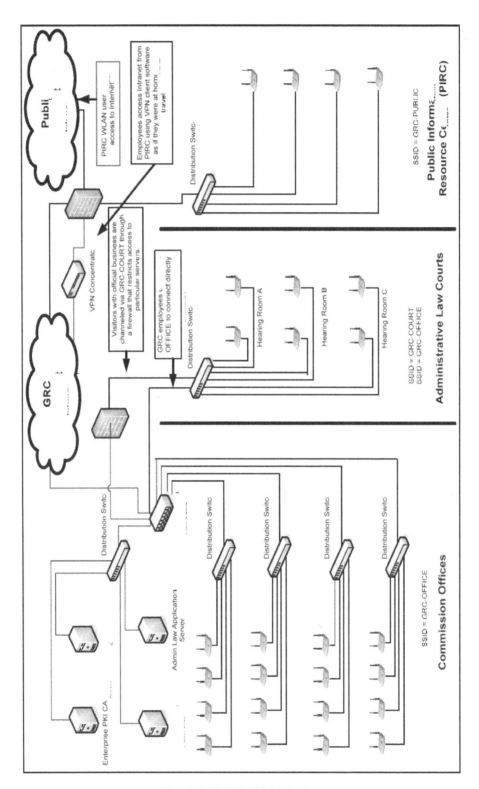

Figure 9-5. GRC WLAN Infrastructure

9.3.3 Summary and Evaluation

The case study reviewed GRC's experience with the initiation and acquisition/development phases of the information systems development life cycle with respect to its WLAN deployment. The commission's objective was to use WLAN technology to improve public access to its information. Its project got off to a strong start largely because it correctly identified when RSNs would facilitate progress towards that objective and when they might not.

The initial GRC analysis led to a high-level design that tailored the RSN strategy for each area in the building based on the level of protection needed given the user community it served. In summary, GRC's main building had three areas that would be supported by WLANs: the commission offices, the administrative law courtrooms, and the Public Information Resource Center.

The solution in the commission offices was similar to WLAN deployments in many organizations, providing users with mobility they did not previously enjoy. The solution for the courtrooms, however, was innovative and greatly expedited the legal administrative processes with which many were frustrated. IEEE 802.11 RSN technology enabled this significant increase in productivity because the judges would not have permitted courtroom network connections without the assurance the RSN provided.

The WLAN solution in the Public Information Resource Center also was an enabling technology, allowing visitors to complete research projects more efficiently than ever before. However, the solution was an open system, providing no link layer security. This configuration at first seemed precarious, but given that the Center's data was public and its WLAN was isolated from other network resources with firewall technology, RSN protections were deemed unnecessary.

This page has been left blank intentionally.

10.   Summary of Concepts and Recommendations

This section summarizes the major concepts and recommendations presented in Sections 2 through 8 of this document. It provides a summary of the major IEEE 802.11 network components and terms, an overview of IEEE 802.11i security, and an introduction to the product certification programs from the Wi-Fi Alliance. It also discusses the operation of a Robust Security Network (RSN) and outlines a recommended life cycle for IEEE 802.11 RSN deployment. Finally, it provides additional recommendations for wireless local area network (WLAN) security.

10.1 IEEE 802.11 Concepts

WLANs usually are implemented as extensions to existing wired LANs, and are used by devices within a fairly limited range, such as an office building. The need for interoperability among different brands of WLAN products led to the development of various WLAN standards. IEEE 802.11 is the dominant WLAN standard. The basic IEEE 802.11 network components and architectural models are as follows:

- **Station (STA).** A *STA* is a wireless endpoint device, such as a laptop, PDA, or mobile phone.

- **Access Point (AP).** An *AP* logically connects STAs with a distribution system, which is typically an organization's wired network infrastructure. APs can also logically connect wireless STAs with each other without accessing a distribution system.

- **Ad Hoc Mode.** This is a wireless network configuration that does not use APs; STAs communicate directly with each other.

- **Independent Basic Service Set (IBSS).** An IBSS is a set of STAs configured in ad hoc mode.

- **Infrastructure Mode.** This wireless network configuration requires APs and is the most commonly used mode for WLANs. An AP connects wireless STAs to each other or to a distribution system.

- **Basic Service Set (BSS).** A BSS is composed of an AP and one or more STAs configured in infrastructure mode. A BSS is the basic building block of a WLAN.

- **Distribution System (DS).** A DS is an infrastructure, typically a wired LAN, that connects individual BSSs to each other.

- **Extended Service Set (ESS).** An ESS is a WLAN comprising more than one BSS connected by a DS.

10.2 IEEE 802.11i Security Overview

Also known as pre-RSN IEEE 802.11, IEEE 802.11 technologies that rely on Wired Equivalent Privacy (WEP) have several well-documented security problems that can be exploited to circumvent or adversely impact access control and authentication, confidentiality, integrity, and availability. To address these, IEEE amended IEEE 802.11 with 802.11i, which was approved in July 2004.

The IEEE 802.11i specification introduces the concept of a Robust Security Network (RSN), which is a wireless network that allows the creation of RSN associations (RSNA) only. RSNAs are logical connections between communicating IEEE 802.11 entities established through the IEEE 802.11i 4-Way Handshake. RSNAs allow for the protection of data frames and provide enhanced security relative to the flawed WEP. RSNAs provide the following security features for IEEE 802.11 WLANs:

- **Enhanced User and Message Authentication Mechanisms.** The Extensible Authentication Protocol (EAP) provides the authentication framework for IEEE 802.11 RSNs that use IEEE 802.1X port-based access control. To accomplish mutual authentication between an AP and a STA, the IEEE 802.1X standard defines an additional entity, an authentication server (AS). IEEE 802.1X allows the client to authenticate to the network through the use of the AS. If the authentication succeeds, the AP receives the resulting Pairwise Master Key (PMK).

  EAP defines the stages of an EAP conversation that includes one or more EAP methods. The EAP methods perform the authentication transaction and generate cryptographic keying material. While the basic rules of the EAP conversation are common to all EAP implementations, the EAP methods can vary from one implementation to another, and EAP can be adapted to new authentication methods as they become available. This flexibility has benefits, but it may also introduce risk. Therefore, organizations should select EAP methods based on a risk assessment of the target environment. Only some EAP methods, such as certain Transport Layer Security-based methods (e.g., EAP-TLS, EAP-Tunneled TLS [EAP-TTLS], Protected EAP [PEAP], can satisfy the security requirements for WLANs.

  Before organizations select WLAN equipment, they should review their existing identity management infrastructure, authentication requirements, and security policy to determine the EAP method or methods that are most appropriate in their environment, then purchase systems that support the chosen EAP methods. Many EAP methods are currently defined only in IETF Internet-drafts and thus are not yet official standards. Organizations are encouraged to obtain the latest available information before making final determinations on their IEEE 802.11 RSN authentication architecture and product procurement.

- **Cryptographic Key Management.** RSNAs use several cryptographic keys to support key generation, encryption, authentication, and integrity functions. The IEEE 802.11i specification defines two key hierarchies for RSNAs: the Pairwise Key Hierarchy, which is designed for unicast data traffic protection, and the Group Key Hierarchy, which is intended for multicast/broadcast traffic protection. In the Pairwise Key Hierarchy, keys may be installed in RSNA devices (ASs and STAs) through two methods:

  - Delivering a pre-shared key (PSK) through an out-of-band mechanism. The IEEE 802.11 standard does not specify how PSKs are to be generated or distributed, so these decisions are left to organizations implementing IEEE 802.11 networks. As a result, organizations should review any PSK approach carefully for possible vulnerabilities and evaluate its performance implications. Distributing PSKs in a large network might be infeasible. The lack of individual user/client authentication in most PSK APs is another reason to avoid the use of pre-shared keys.

  - Delivering an authentication, authorization, and accounting (AAA) key through EAP during authentication. Decisions on the appropriate EAP authentication methods are left to organizations implementing STAs and ASs. As a result, organizations should carefully review any EAP authentication methods for possible vulnerabilities.

  Most organizations choose to implement EAP for authentication instead of using PSKs because of the resources needed for proper PSK administration. EAP authentication requires an organization to use an AS, which may necessitate the use of a public key infrastructure (PKI). Organizations that already have ASs for Web, e-mail, file and print services, and other authentication needs, should consider integrating this technology into their RSN solutions. Most leading network operating systems and directory solutions offer the support needed for RSN integration.

- **Robust Enciphering and Data Integrity Mechanisms.** IEEE 802.11 defines WEP as a data confidentiality and integrity protocol. The IEEE 802.11i amendment defines two additional protocols for RSNAs: Temporal Key Integrity Protocol (TKIP) and Counter Mode with Cipher Block Chaining Message Authentication Code Protocol (CCMP). Federal agencies are required to use Federal Information Processing Standards (FIPS)-approved cryptographic algorithms that are contained in FIPS-validated cryptographic modules. Of WEP, TKIP, and CCMP, only CCMP uses a core cryptographic algorithm that is FIPS-approved, the Advanced Encryption Standard (AES). For other security features, CCMP offers the same or stronger implementations than WEP and TKIP. Accordingly, NIST requires the use of CCMP for securing Federal agencies' IEEE 802.11-based WLANs. For legacy IEEE 802.11 equipment that does not provide CCMP, auxiliary security protection is required; one possibility is the use of an IPsec VPN, using FIPS-approved cryptographic algorithms.

IEEE 802.11i also uses a function known as IEEE 802.1X port-based access control. The IEEE 802.1X framework specified by the IEEE 802.11i amendment provides the means to block user access to the DS until authentication is successful, thereby controlling access to network resources. The technique used to block access is known as port-based access control; it involves the AP distinguishing between EAP and non-EAP frames, then passing EAP frames through an uncontrolled port and non-EAP frames through a controlled port, which can block access.

10.3 Wi-Fi Alliance Product Certification Programs

The Wi-Fi Alliance has established several certification programs to give consumers of WLAN products assurance that their systems comply with IEEE 802.11 specifications and can interoperate with similar equipment from other vendors. The following certifications are available that indicate product compliance with IEEE 802.11i:

- Wi-Fi Protected Access (WPA), which includes a subset of the IEEE 802.11i specification that addresses the weaknesses of WEP

- WPA2, which extends WPA to include the full set of IEEE 802.11i requirements.

Federal agencies should procure WPA2 products that have been FIPS-validated; WPA products cannot be FIPS-validated because they do not support FIPS-approved encryption algorithms. WPA and WPA2 have both Personal and Enterprise modes of operation. Organizations that plan to deploy authentication servers as part of an IEEE 802.1X and EAP implementation should procure products with the Enterprise level certification.

10.4 IEEE 802.11 RSN Operation

IEEE 802.11 RSN operation is based on a frame exchange protocol used to transfer frames between WLAN components—STAs, APs, and ASs. The protocol uses three types of IEEE 802.11 frames, as follows:

- **Data frames**, which encapsulate upper layer protocol packets, including user data (e.g., e-mail, Web pages).

- **Management frames**, which include the management of association and deassociation activities, authentication, probes, and beacons.

- **Control frames**, which are used for requesting and controlling access to the wireless media, such as sending an acknowledgement after receiving a data frame.

By grouping the frame exchanges within the frame exchange protocol by function, IEEE 802.11 RSN operation may be thought of as occurring in five distinct phases:

- **RSN Operation Phase 1: Discovery.** The STA identifies an AP for a WLAN with which it wishes to communicate. The STA locates an AP either by receiving one of the AP's periodic transmissions of Beacon frames, or by sending a Probe Request to solicit a Probe Response from an AP. After the STA has identified an AP, the STA and the AP exchange frames to negotiate various parameters for their communications. By the end of the phase, the STA and AP have agreed on an authentication method.

- **RSN Operation Phase 2: Authentication.** During this phase, the STA and AS prove their identities to each other. The authentication frames pass through the AP, which also blocks non-authentication traffic from the STA using IEEE 802.1X port-based access control. The actual authentication mechanism is implemented by the STA and AS using EAP. EAP provides a framework that allows the use of multiple methods for achieving authentication, including static passwords, dynamic passwords, and public key cryptography certificates. After authentication has been completed, the AAA key is installed in the STA and AS. It serves as a root key to enable the generation of other keys used to secure communications between the STA and AP.

- **RSN Operation Phase 3: Key Generation and Distribution (KGD).** During the KGD phase, the AP and the STA perform several operations that cause cryptographic keys to be generated and placed on the AP and the STA. The KGD phase employs two handshakes: a 4-Way Handshake and a Group Key Handshake. During the 4-Way Handshake, the STA and AP establish a security policy that specifies several key security capabilities, such as data confidentiality and integrity protocols for protecting data traffic, and a key distribution approach. Both handshakes employ message encryption and integrity checking, using one of two confidentiality and integrity algorithms. For both types of handshakes, NIST requires the use of AES Key Wrap with HMAC-SHA-1-128 instead of RC4 encryption with HMAC-MD5 because AES and SHA-1 are FIPS-approved algorithms, and RC4 and MD5 are not. Selecting CCMP as the cipher suite will ensure the use of the appropriate key wrap algorithms.

- **RSN Operation Phase 4: Protected Data Transfer.** The STA and AP share data securely, using the security policy and cryptographic keys established during the first three phases. Because secure data transfer occurs between the STA and the AP only, organizations need to consider carefully the security of the data during the rest of its transit (e.g., on the DS).

- **RSN Operation Phase 5: Connection Termination.** During this phase, the STA and AP tear down their secure connection and delete their association, thereby terminating their wireless connection.

The outcome of the discovery phase is very important to the security posture of a WLAN. In an RSN, an AP should not associate with pre-RSN STAs. If any STAs in a WLAN are using pre-RSN capabilities (e.g., WEP or IEEE 802.11 entity authentication), then those STAs have associations that are not RSNAs. Accordingly, the WLAN is not an RSN, even though many of its STAs might not be using pre-RSN capabilities. Organizations that want to establish IEEE 802.11 RSNs should configure their APs so that they permit the establishment of RSNAs only, not associations based on pre-RSN capabilities. Alternatively, non-RSN STAs should be limited to a separate VLAN where additional controls (e.g. firewalls and FIPS 140-2 validated VPNs) can be applied.

10.5 Life Cycle for IEEE 802.11 RSN Deployment

To be effective, WLAN security should be incorporated throughout the life cycle of WLAN solutions, from policy to operations. The model described in this section is based on one introduced in NIST SP 800-64, *Security Considerations in the Information System Development Life Cycle.* Organizations may follow a project management methodology or life cycle model that does not directly map to the phases in the model presented in this guide, but the types of tasks in the methodology and their sequencing are probably similar. The phases of the life cycle are the following:

- **Deployment Phase 1: Initiation.** This phase includes the tasks to be performed before starting the design of a WLAN solution. These include providing an overall vision for how the WLAN would support the mission of the organization, creating a high-level strategy for the WLAN's implementation, developing a WLAN use policy, and specifying business and functional requirements for the solution.

- **Deployment Phase 2: Acquisition/Development.** For the purposes of this guide, the Acquisition/Development phase is split into the following two parts:

  - **Phase 2a: Planning and Design.** In this phase, WLAN network architects specify the technical characteristics of the WLAN solution and related network components. These characteristics include the EAP method or methods used to support authentication; the protocols used to support communication between client, AP, and AS; access control lists and firewall rules to segregate WLAN traffic; and the nature of the supporting PKI. A site survey is typically conducted to help determine the architecture of the solution.

  - **Phase 2b: Procurement.** This phase involves specifying the number and type of WLAN components that must be purchased, the feature sets they must support, and any certifications they must hold. It may also include procuring client upgrades to support the security policies to be enforced in the WLAN deployment.

- **Deployment Phase 3: Implementation.** In this phase, procured equipment is first configured to meet operational and security requirements, and then it is installed and activated on a production network. Implementation includes altering the configuration of other security controls and technologies, such as security event logging, network management, AAA server integration, and PKI.

- **Deployment Phase 4: Operations/Maintenance.** This phase includes security-related tasks that should be performed on an ongoing basis once the WLAN is operational, including log review and rogue AP detection.

- **Deployment Phase 5: Disposition.** This phase encompasses tasks that occur after a system or its components have been retired, including preserving information to meet legal requirements, sanitizing media, and disposing of equipment properly.

10.6 Additional WLAN Security Recommendations

In addition to the recommendations presented throughout Sections 3 through 7 of this document, Section 8 provides over 50 best practice recommendations for WLAN security, grouped by the life cycle phase for which each recommendation is most relevant.[122] Organizations are strongly encouraged to adopt the "best practice" recommendations. Failure to implement them significantly increases the risk of a WLAN

---

[122] For the sake of brevity, the recommendations are not duplicated in this section Readers should consult Tables 8-1 through 8-6 for the recommended best practices for each life cycle phase

security breach. Organizations should also examine each of the "should consider" recommendations to determine their applicability to the target environment. In general, "should consider" recommendations enhance security beyond what can be achieved through the "best practice" recommendations. A "should consider" recommendation should be rejected only if it is infeasible or if the reduction in risk from its implementation does not justify its cost.

WLANs face several types of high-level threats, including denial of service attacks, eavesdropping, man-in-the-middle attacks, masquerading, message modification, message replay, and traffic analysis. WLAN threats most commonly involve an attacker with access to the radio link between two STAs or between a STA and an AP. Implementing the recommendations presented in this guide for a new or existing WLAN should help to provide reasonable assurance that an organization is protected against most WLAN security threats. In addition, organizations should use guidance on general security controls, such as the recommendations presented in NIST SP 800-53 for minimum management, operational, and technical security controls for information systems.

11. Future Directions

As the IEEE 802.11 protocol is used in increasingly diverse and demanding environments, additional requirements appear that necessitate extensions to the IEEE 802.11i security measures. Timelines for these, and other 802.11 standards, can be found at http://grouper.ieee.org/groups/802/11/Reports/802.11_Timelines.htm. Currently, there are two IEEE 802.11 Working Groups that are addressing security-related standards.

11.1 IEEE 802.11r: Fast Roaming/Fast BSS Transition

When an IEEE 802.11 wireless LAN is used to support the connection to a voice terminal, each time a wireless device moves enough to require a transition from one AP to another, this necessitates a new authentication exchange as well as another 4-Way Handshake. These exchanges can result in latency severe enough to cause a call to be dropped or at the very least to appear unresponsive. Even the use of Pre-Authentication and PMKSA caching are not enough to solve this problem. IEEE 802.11 Task Group R was formed to define a secure mechanism that will enable more rapid transitions. Completion of the IEEE 802.11r standard is targeted for March 2007.

11.2 IEEE 802.11w: Protected Management Frames

IEEE 802.11i added effective security protections to IEEE 802.11 wireless communications. However, those protections are only provided for data frames exchanged by a STA and an AP. This leaves another category of communications, management frames, vulnerable to attack and manipulation by unauthorized parties. Those management frames that are exchanged before authentication and key establishment take place cannot be protected, since the requisite security mechanisms have not yet been put into place. Other management frames (e.g., deauthentication and disassociation) could make use of the IEEE 802.11 RSNA for protection. Without this protection, an adversary could inject these management frames, causing a STA to be unwillingly removed from the wireless network. Defining the mechanisms to provide this protection is the motivation behind the formation of IEEE 802.11 Task Group W. 802.11w has gone to letter ballot, the first major milestone in becoming a standard; completion of the IEEE 802.11w standard is targeted for March 2008.

This page has been left blank intentionally.

Appendix A—Acronyms

Selected acronyms used in *Establishing Wireless Robust Security Networks: A Guide to IEEE 802.11i* are defined below.

AAA	Authentication, Authorization, and Accounting
AAAK	Authentication, Authorization, and Accounting Key
AAD	Additional Authentication Data
ACL	Access Control List
AES	Advanced Encryption Standard
AKM	Authentication and Key Management
AP	Access Point
AS	Authentication Server
ATIM	Announcement Traffic Indication Message
AVP	Attribute-Value Pair
BSS	Basic Service Set
BSSID	Basic Service Set Identifier
CA	Certification Authority
CBC	Cipher Block Chaining
CBC-MAC	Cipher Block Chaining Message Authentication Code
CCM	Counter Mode with Cipher Block Chaining (CBC) Message Authentication Code (MAC)
CCMP	Counter Mode with Cipher Block Chaining (CBC) Message Authentication Code (MAC) Protocol
CHAP	Challenge-Handshake Authentication Protocol
CIO	Chief Information Officer
CRC	Cyclic Redundancy Check
DA	Destination Address
DS	Distribution System
EAP	Extensible Authentication Protocol
EAP-FAST	Extensible Authentication Protocol Flexible Authentication via Secure Tunneling
EAP-TLS	Extensible Authentication Protocol-Transport Layer Security
EAP-TTLS	Extensible Authentication Protocol-Tunneled Transport Layer Security
EAPOL	Extensible Authentication Protocol Over LAN
EAPOL-KCK	Extensible Authentication Protocol Over LAN Key Confirmation Key
EAPOL-KEK	Extensible Authentication Protocol Over LAN Key Encryption Key
EMSK	Extended Master Session Key
ESS	Extended Service Set
ETSI	European Telecommunications Standards Institute
FCS	Frame Check Sequence
FIPS	Federal Information Processing Standards
FISMA	Federal Information Security Management Act
FMS	Fluhrer-Mantin-Shamir
GHz	Gigahertz
GMK	Group Master Key
GRS	General Records Schedule

GTC	Generic Token Card
GTK	Group Temporal Key
HIPERLAN	High Performance Radio Local Area Network
HMAC	Hash Message Authentication Code
IANA	Internet Assigned Numbers Authority
IBSS	Independent Basic Service Set
ICV	Integrity Check Value
IEEE	Institute of Electrical and Electronics Engineers
IETF	Internet Engineering Task Force
IKE	Internet Key Exchange
IP	Internet Protocol
IPsec	Internet Protocol Security
ITL	Information Technology Laboratory
IV	Initialization Vector
Kbps	Kilobit per second
KGD	Key Generation and Distribution
LAN	Local Area Network
LDAP	Lightweight Directory Access Protocol
MAC	Media Access Control
MAC	Message Authentication Code
Mbps	Megabit per second
MD	Message Digest
MHz	Megahertz
MIC	Message Integrity Code
MOU	Memorandum of Understanding
MS-CHAP	Microsoft Challenge-Handshake Authentication Protocol
MSK	Master Session Key
MTU	Maximum Transmission Unit
NIC	Network Interface Card
NIST	National Institute of Standards and Technology
NTP	Network Time Protocol
OMB	Office of Management and Budget
OTP	One-Time Password
PAC	Protected Access Credential
PDA	Personal Digital Assistant
PEAP	Protected Extensible Authentication Protocol
PIN	Personal Identification Number
PKI	Public Key Infrastructure
PMK	Pairwise Master Key
PMKSA	Pairwise Master Key Security Association
PN	Packet Number
PPP	Point-to-Point Protocol
PRF	Pseudo-Random Function

PSK	Pre-shared Key
PTK	Pairwise Transient Key
PUB	Publication
RA	Receiver Address
RADIUS	Remote Authentication Dial In User Service
RFC	Request for Comment
RSN	Robust Security Network
RSNA	Robust Security Network Association
RSNIE	Robust Security Network Information Element
SA	Source Address
SHA	Secure Hash Algorithm
SHS	Secure Hash Standard
SIM	Subscriber Identity Module
SiPS	Signal Processing System
SNMP	Simple Network Management Protocol
SP	Special Publication
SSH	Secure Shell
SSID	Service Set Identifier
SSL	Secure Sockets Layer
STA	Station
TA	Transmitter Address
TK	Temporal Key
TKIP	Temporal Key Integrity Protocol
TLS	Transport Layer Security
TSC	TKIP Sequence Counter
TSN	Transition Security Network
TTLS	Tunneled Transport Layer Security
USB	Universal Serial Bus
UWB	Ultrawideband
VLAN	Virtual Local Area Network
VPN	Virtual Private Network
WEP	Wired Equivalent Privacy
Wi-Fi	Wireless Fidelity
WLAN	Wireless Local Area Network
WMAN	Wireless Metropolitan Area Network
WMM	Wi-Fi Multimedia
WPA	Wi-Fi Protected Access
WPAN	Wireless Personal Area Network
WWAN	Wireless Wide Area Network

This page has been left blank intentionally.

Appendix B—References

Altunbasak, Hayriye and Owen, Henry, "Alternative Pair-wise Key Exchange Protocols for Robust Security Networks (IEEE 802.11i) in Wireless LANs", IEEE SOUTHEASTCON, 2004.

Anderson, Gustave et al, "A Secure Wireless Agent-based Testbed", *Proceedings of the Second IEEE International Information Assurance Workshop*, 2004.

Baghaei, Nilufar and Hunt, Ray, "IEEE 802.11 Wireless LAN Security Performance Using Multiple Clients", *Proceedings of the 12th IEEE International Conference on Networks*, 2004.

Bargh, Mortaza et al, "Fast Authentication Methods for Handovers Between IEEE 802.11 Wireless LANs", *Proceedings of the 2nd ACM International Workshop on Wireless Mobile Applications and Services on WLAN Hotspots*, 2004.

Becker, Bernd, Eisinger, Jochen, and Winterer, Peter, "Securing Wireless Networks in a University Environment", *Proceedings of the Third IEEE International Conference on Pervasive Computing and Communications Workshops*, 2005.

Carli, Marco, Neri, A., and Rossetti, A., "Integrated Security Architecture for WLAN", *Proceedings of the IEEE 10th International Conference on Telecommunications*, 2003.

Chen, Jyh-Cheng, Jiang, Ming-Chia, and Liu, Yi-Wen, "Wireless LAN Security and IEEE 802.11i", *IEEE Wireless Communications*, February 2005.

Chen, Jyh-Cheng, Liu, Yi-Wen, and Wang, Yu-Ping, "Design and Implementation of WIRE1x", *Proceedings of Taiwan Area Network Conference*, 2003.

Edney, Jon and Arbaugh, William A., *Real 802.11 Security: Wi-Fi Protected Access and 802.11i*, Addison-Wesley, 2004.

Fluhrer, Scott, Mantin, Itsik, and Shamir, Adi, "Weaknesses in the Key Schedule Algorithm of RC4", *Proceedings of the 4th Annual Workshop on Selected Areas of Cryptography*, 2001.

Gast, Matthew S., *802.11® Wireless Networks: The Definitive Guide (2nd Edtion)*, O'Reilly Media, 2005.

He, Changhua, and Mitchell, John, "Analysis of the 802.11i 4-Way Handshake", *Proceedings of the 2004 ACM Workshop on Wireless Security*, 2004.

IEEE Standard 802.11, 1999 Edition. Also available at http://standards.ieee.org/getieee802/download/802.11-1999.pdf.

IEEE Standard 802.11i, 2004 Edition. Also available at http://standards.ieee.org/getieee802/download/802.11i-2004.pdf.

IEEE Standard 802.1X, 2004 Edition. Also available at http://standards.ieee.org/getieee802/download/802.1X-2004.pdf.

Matsunaga, Yasuhiko et al, "Secure Authentication System for Public WLAN Roaming", *Proceedings of the First ACM International Workshop on Wireless Mobile Applications and Services on WLAN Hotspots*, 2003.

Mitsuyama, Yukio et al, "Embedded Architecture of IEEE 802.11i Cipher Algorithms", *Proceedings of the IEEE International Symposium on Consumer Electronics*, 2004.

O'Hara, Bob and Petrick, Al, *IEEE 802.11 Handbook: A Designer's Companion*, IEEE Press, 2001.

Schmoyer, Tim, Lim, Yu-Xi, and Owen, Henry, "Wireless Intrusion Detection and Response: A Case Study Using the Classic Man-in-the-middle Attack", *Proceedings of IEEE Wireless Communication and Networking Conference 2004,* 2004.

Smyth, Neil, McLoone, Máire, and McCanny, John, "Reconfigurable Hardware Acceleration of WLAN Security", *IEEE Workshop on Signal Processing Systems (SiPS) Design & Implementation*, 2004.

Šorman, Matija, Kovač, Tomislav, and Maurović, Damir, "Implementing Improved WLAN Security", *46th International Symposium Electronics in Marine*, 2004.

Wool, Avishai, "A Note on the Fragility of the 'Michael' Message Integrity Code", *IEEE Transactions on Wireless Communications*, Vol. 3 No. 5, September 2004.

You, Liyu and Jamshaid, Kamran, "Novel Applications for 802.11x Enabled Wireless Networked Home", *2004 IEEE Consumer Communications and Networking Conference*, 2004.

Appendix C—Online Resources

This section lists online resources that may be helpful for better understanding IEEE 802.11 RSNs and the IEEE 802.11i amendment.

Documents

Name	URL
Deploying Wi-Fi Protected Access (WPA™) and WPA2™ in the Enterprise	http://www.wi-fi.org/white_papers/whitepaper-022705-deployingwpawpa2enterprise/
EAP Registry	http://www.iana.org/assignments/eap-numbers
FIPS 140-2, Security Requirements for Cryptographic Modules	http://csrc.nist.gov/publications/fips/fips140-2/fips1402.pdf
FIPS 180-2, Secure Hash Standard (SHS)	http://csrc.nist.gov/publications/fips/fips180-2/fips180-2withchangenotice.pdf
FIPS 197, Advanced Encryption Standard	http://csrc.nist.gov/publications/fips/fips197/fips-197.pdf
FIPS 199, Standards for Security Categorization of Federal Information and Information Systems	http://csrc.nist.gov/publications/fips/fips199/FIPS-PUB-199-final.pdf
GRS 24, Information Technology Operations and Management Records	http://www.archives.gov/records-mgmt/ardor/grs24.html
Michael: An Improved MIC for 002.11 WEP	http://grouper.ieee.org/groups/802/11/Documents/DocumentHolder/2-020.zip
NIST SP 800-30, Risk Management Guide for Information Technology Systems	http://csrc.nist.gov/publications/nistpubs/800-30/sp800-30.pdf
NIST SP 800-32, Introduction to Public Key Technology and the Federal PKI Infrastructure	http://csrc.nist.gov/publications/nistpubs/800-32/sp800-32.pdf
NIST SP 800-40 version 2, Creating a Patch and Vulnerability Management Program	http://csrc.nist.gov/publications/nistpubs/800-40-Ver2/SP800-40v2.pdf
NIST SP 800-41, Guidelines on Firewalls and Firewall Policy	http://csrc.nist.gov/publications/nistpubs/800-41/sp800-41.pdf
NIST SP 800-48, Wireless Network Security: 802.11, Bluetooth and Handheld Devices	http://csrc.nist.gov/publications/nistpubs/800-48/NIST_SP_800-48.pdf
NIST SP 800-50, Building an Information Technology Security Awareness and Training Program	http://csrc.nist.gov/publications/nistpubs/800-50/NIST-SP800-50.pdf
NIST SP 800-52, Guidelines for the Selection and Use of Transport Layer Security (TLS) Implementations	http://csrc.nist.gov/publications/nistpubs/800-52/SP800-52.pdf
NIST SP 800-53 Revision 1, Recommended Security Controls for Federal Information Systems	http://csrc.nist.gov/publications/nistpubs/800-53-Rev1/800-53-rev1-final-clean-sz.pdf
NIST SP 800-63, Electronic Authentication Guideline	http://csrc.nist.gov/publications/nistpubs/800-63/SP800-63V1_0_2.pdf
NIST SP 800-64, Security Considerations in the Information System Development Life Cycle	http://csrc.nist.gov/publications/nistpubs/800-64/NIST-SP800-64.pdf
NIST SP 800-70, Security Configuration Checklists Program for IT Products – Guidance for Checklists Users and Developers	http://checklists.nist.gov/docs/SP_800-70_20050526.pdf
NIST SP 800-77, Guide to IPsec VPNs	http://csrc.nist.gov/publications/nistpubs/800-77/sp800-77.pdf
NIST SP 800-94, Guide to Intrusio n Detection and Prevention Systems (IDPS)	http://csrc.nist.gov/publications/nistpubs/800-94/SP800-94.pdf

Name	URL
The DoD Public Key Infrastructure and Public Key-Enabling Frequently Asked Questions	http://iase.disa.mil/pki/faq-pki-pke-may-2004.doc
Wi-Fi Protected Access (WPA) Enhanced Security Implementation Based on IEEE P802.11i standard, Version 3.1	http://www.wi-fi.org/OpenSection/protected_access.asp (obtained from a link on this site for a fee)

Resource Sites

Name	URL
FIPS-validated Cryptographic Modules	http://csrc.nist.gov/cryptval/
IEEE 802.11 working group information	http://grouper.ieee.org/groups/802/11/QuickGuide_IEEE_802_WG_and_Activities.htm
International Engineering Consortium	http://www.iec.org/online/tutorials/eap_methods/
NIST's Security Configuration Checklists Program for IT Products	http://csrc.nist.gov/pcig/
SNMP	http://www.snmp.com/snmpv3/
Wi-Fi Alliance	http://www.wi-fi.org/
Wi-Fi Alliance Certified WLAN Systems	http://www.wi-fi.org/OpenSection/certification_programs.asp?TID=2

Request for Comment (RFC) Documents

Name	URL
RFC 1994, *PPP Challenge Handshake Authentication Protocol (CHAP)*	http://www.ietf.org/rfc/rfc1994.txt
RFC 2104, *HMAC: Keyed-Hashing for Message Authentication*	http://www.ietf.org/rfc/rfc2104.txt
RFC 2243, *OTP Extended Responses*	http://www.ietf.org/rfc/rfc2243.txt
RFC 2246, *The TLS Protocol, Version 1.0*	http://www.ietf.org/rfc/rfc2246.txt
RFC 2284, *PPP Extensible Authentication Protocol (EAP)*	http://www.ietf.org/rfc/rfc2284.txt
RFC 2289, *A One-Time Password System*	http://www.ietf.org/rfc/rfc2289.txt
RFC 2716, *PPP EAP TLS Authentication Protocol*	http://www.ietf.org/rfc/rfc2716.txt
RFC 2828, *Internet Security Glossary*	http://www.ietf.org/rfc/rfc2828.txt
RFC 2865, *RADIUS*	http://www.ietf.org/rfc/rfc2865.txt
RFC 2869, *RADIUS Extensions*	http://www.ietf.org/rfc/rfc2869.txt
RFC 3394, *Advanced Encryption Standard (AES) Key Wrap Algorithm*	http://www.ietf.org/rfc/rfc3394.txt
RFC 3546, *Transport Layer Security (TLS) Extensions*	http://www.ietf.org/rfc/rfc3546.txt
RFC 3579, *RADIUS Support for EAP*	http://www.ietf.org/rfc/rfc3579.txt
RFC 3580, *IEEE 802.1X Remote Authentication Dial In User Service (RADIUS) Usage Guidelines*	http://www.ietf.org/rfc/rfc3580.txt
RFC 3588, *Diameter Base Protocol*	http://www.ietf.org/rfc/rfc3588.txt
RFC 3610, *Counter with CBC-MAC (CCM)*	http://www.ietf.org/rfc/rfc3610.txt
RFC 3748, *Extensible Authentication Protocol (EAP)*	http://www.ietf.org/rfc/rfc3748.txt
RFC 4017, *Extensible Authentication Protocol (EAP) Method Requirements for Wireless LANs*	http://www.ietf.org/rfc/rfc4017.txt
RFC 4306, *Internet Key Exchange (IKEv2) Protocol*	http://www.ietf.org/rfc/rfc4306.txt

www.ingramcontent.com/pod-product-compliance
Lightning Source LLC
Chambersburg PA
CBHW080419060326

40689CB00019B/4295